T0392398

"Ranging across fields, one of a kind, Gustafson seems to have invented himself. Intuitive, lightning quick, swimming in the flow of the unconscious, he drops an interpretation into a supersaturated brew, and what will crystalize awaits us. Collaborative, humane, he listens – pivots – and self-corrects his canny/uncanny flashes by literally sleeping on it, dreaming his way into recrystallizing awareness. This dreamy book is terse and telegraphic, perhaps edgy, but always creative and evocative."

Alfred Margulies, MD, author of The Empathic Imagination;
Harvard Medical School

"In a style that is both erudite and conversational Gustafson illuminates the power of the unconscious and its manifestation through dreams. Interweaving brief narratives of his patients with their dreams and his own, the depth of his wisdom and professional experience as well as breath of scholarship and candid self-disclosure result in a rich read. It is a very impressive contribution to our understanding of the unconscious and the role of dreams to guide our patients and to inspire us with its dimensions of beauty, creativity and ultimately the sacred."

Jonathan D. Smith, LLb, CQSW, UKCP registered. Clinical Service Lead for Staff Counselling & Well-being, South London & Maudsley NHS Trust

"Gustafson shows us how each patient arrives at the office, stuck in a critical dilemma, i.e., to stay with a controlling husband or not, then what? He describes frequently brief treatments, in which he often follows the patient's dreams, and his own dreams, in reaction, to develop a 'second impression' of the issue, deeper than the manifest content of the initial request. This new information is often in a pictorial dream form and not in a verbal linear one, direct communications from the unconscious. Dr Gustafson shows how the treatments framed by W. Reich, H.S Sullivan and D.W. Winnicott pivot on a similar construction of the 'second impression.' Gustafson is a brilliant scholar of psychotherapy's historical sweep. This volume represents a true second impression of the world we thought we knew so well and is a crucial addition to any therapists outlook."

Jim Donovan PhD., Associate Professor of Population Medicine (Part Time), Harvard Medical School

"I love reading Gustafson! He is highly intelligent, literary, and I always come away with new perspectives and interesting ideas. *The Importance of Second Impressions in Psychotherapy* offers the advantage of ways to anticipate and handle conflicts and dilemmas. As carpenters say, 'measure twice, cut once.' Highly recommended!"

Michael F. Hoyt, Ph.D., author/editor of Brief Therapy and Beyond: Therapist Stories of Inspiration, Passion, and Renewal; Single-Session Therapy by Walk-In or Appointment; *and* Creative Therapy in Challenging Situations: Unusual Interventions to Help Clients

Gaining a Second Impression in Psychotherapy

Integrating psychotherapy with psychoanalysis and philosophy, this text offers therapists a way to reframe a client's understanding of their mental health issues through a holistic, dynamic lens.

Drawing from theory, research and over fifty years of clinical practice, Dr. Gustafson analyzes a unique range of case stories from diverse clients with varying problems including trauma, anxiety, depression, stress and relationship conflict. This book pictures five different domains that make huge differences in the quality of psychotherapy. Part I offers a snapshot of what is possible for the patient during the initial patient study. Part II shows how the patient's expectations can be subverted. Part III draws upon subconscious elements, mainly dreams, that can provide the patient with unique perspectives that the conscious mind is not capable of. In Part IV, the author looks at how the evolution of human emotions and relationships can have a negative impact on the individual patient. Part V examines the impact that large-scale issues such as religion and faith can have upon our daily lives.

The author weaves together philosophical theory, psychoanalytic techniques and psychodynamic psychotherapeutic strategies, to provide clinicians and therapists with an innovative approach to healing their clients.

James Gustafson is a Professor of Psychiatry at the University of Wisconsin and the author of thirteen books on psychotherapy, including *Very Brief Psychotherapy*, *The Complex Secret of Brief Psychotherapy* and *The Dilemmas of Brief Psychotherapy*. He is a graduate of Harvard College with AB and of Harvard Medical School with MD.

Gaining a Second Impression in Psychotherapy

Pivoting Toward a More Accurate Understanding of the Patient

James Gustafson

NEW YORK AND LONDON

First published 2020
by Routledge
52 Vanderbilt Avenue, New York, NY 10017

and by Routledge
2 Park Square, Milton Park, Abingdon, Oxon, OX14 4RN

Routledge is an imprint of the Taylor & Francis Group, an informa business

© 2020 Taylor & Francis

The right of James Gustafson to be identified as author of this work has been asserted by him in accordance with sections 77 and 78 of the Copyright, Designs and Patents Act 1988.

All rights reserved. No part of this book may be reprinted or reproduced or utilized in any form or by any electronic, mechanical, or other means, now known or hereafter invented, including photocopying and recording, or in any information storage or retrieval system, without permission in writing from the publishers.

Trademark notice: Product or corporate names may be trademarks or registered trademarks, and are used only for identification and explanation without intent to infringe.

Library of Congress Cataloging-in-Publication Data
Names: Gustafson, James Paul, author.
Title: Gaining a second impression in psychotherapy : pivoting toward a more accurate understanding of the patient / James Gustafson.
Description: New York, NY : Routledge, 2020. | Includes bibliographical references and index. |
Identifiers: LCCN 2019051074 (print) | LCCN 2019051075 (ebook)
| ISBN 9780367259365 (hardback) | ISBN 9780367281250
(paperback) | ISBN 9780429299766 (ebook)
Subjects: LCSH: Psychotherapy. | Psychoanalysis and philosophy. |
Psychotherapist and patient. | Mind and body.
Classification: LCC RC480 .G87 2020 (print) | LCC RC480 (ebook)
| DDC 616.89/14–dc23
LC record available at https://lccn.loc.gov/2019051074
LC ebook record available at https://lccn.loc.gov/2019051075

ISBN: 978-0-367-25936-5 (hbk)
ISBN: 978-0-367-28125-0 (pbk)
ISBN: 978-0-429-29976-6 (ebk)

Typeset in Bembo
by Wearset Ltd, Boldon, Tyne and Wear

To invent is to choose – **Henri Poincaré (1910)**

Contents

Preface		xi
Acknowledgements		xiii
PART I: Focus		**1**
Chapter 1	What Is Possible And What Is Not Possible	3
Chapter 2	Forces In Shadow	9
Chapter 3	Dilemmas	13
PART II: Reversals		**19**
Chapter 4	Life Lies	21
Chapter 5	Will Trying To Do The Work Of The Imagination	27
Chapter 6	Double Takes	35
PART III: Dreams and Myths As Second Impression		**43**
Chapter 7	The Pivot Of The Night Painting As Second Impression	45
Chapter 8	A Step From Walking Off A Cliff	55
Chapter 9	Imagining What Has Not Been Imagined	65
PART IV: The Evolution Of The Species In Everyday Life		**71**
Chapter 10	How Our Species Came To Love Acceleration In Jumps	73
Chapter 11	Dangerous Intersections Of Evolution In Everyday Life	79

| Chapter 12 | Brakes Are Necessary If You Are To See The Whole Situation | 85 |

PART V: The Great World In Everyday Life — **93**

Chapter 13	The Immense Realm Of The False	95
Chapter 14	Noble Playing Fields	101
Chapter 15	Religious Deliverance: Light And Dark	105

Afterword — 113

Index — 115

Preface

Your advantage in reading this book could be that you will see how a single picture can help you to think. This is because a single picture can pose an important problem. All the original science like that of Einstein, Poincaré and Kekulé worked this way. My fifteen chapters are such pictures. They provide a pivot that imagines what is going wrong and how it might go right instead. It looks backward and forward, pivoting between the two.

As I compose this book I notice that it is all about stories and how they turn out. The subjects are many in your education, but they all have to do with pivoting between *1st* and *2nd* impressions. I refer to stories of amazement, of hidden forces, of dilemmas, of attractive things that can go afoul, of will that lacks imagination, of double takes that make admiring dangerous, of night paintings, of what the unconscious cares about, of originality or second birth that is selected by a sieve, of accelerating like a hot engine, of intersections that can kill you or not, of too much information and brakes on it, of the immense realm of the false versus the hierarchy of aims, of the delight and vulnerability of play, of lifelines for reading light and dark that can save us or snare us, of being beguiled by surfaces or taking one's time to penetrate them.

I always said to my Door County Symposium colleagues since 1993 that they are the orchestra and I am merely the conductor. They know the stories already, but often do not know that they know the music. It is such delight to find it.

As for the method of my composing this book, I first wrote out its five parts with three chapters each briefly, with the core idea of each one. This set up my unconscious to reply with what more needs to be developed. Like Poincaré in his essay, "Mathematical creation" (1910), I have waited for my sieve to point to the starting point that needs further development in each of the chapters.

There are many different stories. What is the Story of stories (Michael Wood, personal communication)? It is the Story of 2nd Impressions. Only from the 2nd impressions do we comprehend the whole situations.

These 2nd impressions are pictures that allow us to think about what we want and what we don't want (Freire, 1970). They are all analogies or metaphors. That is, they are not literally true. They are analogous to what we want and don't want.

A friend (Gary Simoneau, personal communication) gave me a startling example. "I was looking out the window with my old girlfriend beside me. Two swans were doing a loop-de-loop – just beautiful. Then they turned into fighter jets on the second loop. I decided against asking out the new woman." This way of thinking, comparing the 1st impression to a 2nd impression, has a great economy of energy. This is the Story of stories.

References

Freire, P.: *Pedagogy of the Oppressed*. New York: Herder and Herder, 1970.
Poincaré, H.: Mathematical creation. *The Monist*, XX, July 3, 1910.

Acknowledgements

My thanks to Ruth Gustafson, Gary Simoneau and Mike Wood for their helpful readings of most of the book, which I remain responsible for.

My thanks also to Ryan Ashton for his valuable IT assistance.

Focus

Chapter 1   What Is Possible And What Is Not Possible

Chapter 2   Forces In Shadow

Chapter 3   Dilemmas

What Is Possible And What Is Not Possible

Your advantage in reading this chapter could be your readiness to hear the tone of amazement in your own voice. You may remember I told you that it signifies the following sentence: "I cannot believe this is happening again." Well, it is happening again, so you might as well be ready for it.

Many patients look to find the ideal. For example, a graduate student went to Mexico to study Spanish intensively, being sure it would be great. It was actually terrible. The lessons were poor. The students were rich kids looking to take trips every weekend. Her roommate talked about our patient to the rich kids. Tension built slowly by weeks until she awoke at 3 AM with the sensation that her heart had stopped and then just jumped out of her chest.

It turned out that her conviction that her moves should have great results had a long history of great hopes turning into unbearable pain. She needed my help to comprehend the entire series of being thwarted, set in motion by great expectations. She had been living a myth of her omnipotence.

In other words, some patients need depth of understanding in order to see how their idealizing that things will be great will keep getting them in trouble. On the other hand, some patients see too much of what is painful. They need comforting details to go on at all.

Couples therapy is another such place to be clear about what is possible and what is not. I had a patient whose husband seemed to have to control everything. She could not bear it. He seemed to feel that she never gave him a chance to be helpful.

I said to her that maybe she was not giving him a chance? She thought and thought and could come up with nothing she could do. We were about to finish our session. Somehow she got talking about how small their house was. She felt she could never be alone with her thoughts and feelings in her own house. When she took to her kitchen to clear it up and make supper, her husband always came in to help her.

I said to her that she could give her husband a chance. She could tell him she wanted the kitchen to herself. "Can I?" She said. I replied: "Is it possible to have a room of one's own?" That seemed right to her. That detail made a big difference to her.

It is time to go back to Freud and Breuer in *Studies on Hysteria* (1895) to see what they saw. Then we can see successively what their successors saw.

Freud and Breuer told of what they saw in five patients, all women. They saw women subjugated to men holding all the power in Victorian Vienna. For example, Lucy came to Freud complaining of the smell of burnt pudding that would not go away. Freud's instinct was to follow the trail of this smell to where it happened. Lucy was a governess for two children of a man whose wife had died. Lucy's hopes were to be the next wife since the two children were devoted to her. He would be grateful. Alas, he would not. Just as she was making pudding for the children, the father let her know that she would not be the next wife. That is how Lucy forgot the pudding she was making. It was burned. The stench was in her nose.

Lucy could not say on her own, without Freud, what had befallen her. As Freud and Breuer wrote in the conclusion of their book, these five women were self-strangulated. Freud helped Lucy remove the noose from her neck.

Wilhelm Reich was Freud's favorite in the 1920s. He was the training analyst in the Vienna Psychoanalytic Institute and published his findings in his book called *Character Analysis* (1933). He saw something that was not seen by Freud. He saw the character armor that assembled all the lesser defenses under a constant attitude, such as having to be nice. This limitation would make things like rage impossible. Of course, being subordinated and subjugated as women would tend to smolder more and more and not find a voice.

Sullivan in his *Clinical Studies in Psychiatry* (1956) saw things differently with his women patients as in the case of the housewife economist. She had a PhD in economics like her husband, but just stayed miserable and apathetic as a housewife.

Sullivan saw her as vastly underemployed. He said in his lecture that he was determined to help raise her sights about her potential. Why not economics? Sullivan saw her husband not as oppressing her. He was not a bad guy. It was a matter of the wife seeing her potential and gradually giving herself more interesting things to do using her intelligence. She would gradually see that she did not have to remain miserable and apathetic.

Sullivan was a master at seeing what was possible and what was not possible. He would not suggest a wild goose chase. After all, there are husbands that are bastards. To encourage a wife to challenge him would be dangerous. Sullivan could look at the world beside his patient and judge its potential and lack of potential accurately with her.

Now I am quite aware that there were many more masters of seeing what the patient has not been able to see. I am thinking of Jung and Alexander and French and Balint much later.

I would like next to consider how D.W. Winnicott saw his patients as portrayed in *Therapeutic Consultations in Child Psychiatry* (1971) and *The Piggle* (1977). Winnicott saw his consultations with children as a sacred event. He would see the child when the parents had spoken of him enough times. The children who came to visit him would often have had a dream of his being the doctor that he or she needed.

His interviews were generally what Winnicott called the squiggle game. He would make a mark with a crayon and ask the child to complete it. After the child did complete it, Winnicott would ask her to say what she saw. At the start, the child saw conventional objects like dolls and houses. The child then made a mark first and Winnicott completed it. He would ask what the child saw in their shared drawing. Again the child would see something conventional. So they went on taking turns making the first mark.

At some point in the game, Winnicott would feel the interview was hanging fire at he put it. He called this the moment of the dream drop. He would say casually to the child something like this: "I bet you have dreamed about this." Often the child would nod and tell it.

In other words, Winnicott had found a way to get the help from the unconscious as a 2nd impression. The dream would be uncanny in going to the situation in which the child had lost faith and thus lost her lifeline. Often this happened when a younger child was born and the mother would be preoccupied with him. The unspoken disaster was that the child patient had lost her mother. Winnicott and the child would see it together for what it was, a disaster, yes, but now a shared disaster that was not so overwhelming.

So the focus had another possibility with Winnicott that was not seen with Freud, Reich or Sullivan. All four of these doctors gave their company to the patients with the pain that made it less overwhelming. This was the common thread to enter the labyrinth of the past gone wrong, to enter it together and then to come back out together with new potential. Freud gave his company to the smell of burnt pudding as a neurological symptom, Reich to the smolder of rage under the nice constant attitude, Sullivan to the potential of an interesting life as an economist and now Winnicott to the dream drop where the disaster happened.

As for me, I love having these four ways to be company for the hurt patient. I find it moving and even thrilling.

Seeing differently from amazed patients can make a big difference. When they are amazed they are actually saying: "I cannot believe this is happening." It is happening. It can be spelled out. I often see one such patient after another. Each plays a sequence that is harmful for him or her. The first I saw was bored with too little work. When he took on more he was suddenly swamped by far too much. The second compared himself to illustrious people and of course felt inadequate. The third was about being bulldozed by his big brother he really could get away from.

Each could see that he could refrain from the sequence that was bad for him. Sullivan (1956) taught me this. Sullivan called it selective inattention. The remedy is careful precise attention.

Unselfishness as a virtue sees selfishness as evil. Of course it could be evil. But unselfishness by itself gets run over. I like to say to unselfish patients they are poorly defended. I like to ask them what they are going to do for themselves? It often turns out that they have already begun.

One such patient liked to be in my office for all the pictures of animals. She liked the wolves the most, especially the one staring right at her. She commented to me that that wolf could be her totem animal. She told me why. "He looks right at you straight out and asks nothing of you." This is what she wished people were like. This is not what people are like. They asked way too much of her. She had better be prepared to say no. She needed a lot of practice with the word no. Once again we come across what is possible with people and what is mostly not possible. Wolves are different.

I had a patient who noticed that she did many things like her mother and she did not like what she saw. She noticed that she mostly acted entitled to be taken care of without lifting a finger. She felt it was high time to take care of the household herself.

This 2nd impression was an opportunity, a picture of a pivot, to begin going in another direction. I asked her how she was going to do it? She replied that a friend told her she might make a list every day in the priority or order she would work. She liked that idea and she liked herself much more. She respected herself more.

She saw in one glance that it was possible to go on being entitled like her mother that she did not respect, but it was also possible to pivot to go in this different direction to begin taking care of her household quite unlike her mother. This is what I meant in my Preface about a picture that poses a problem and brings it to an absolute clarity of focus.

References

Freud, S. and Breuer, J.: *Studies on Hysteria* (1895). London: Hogarth Press, 1955.

Reich, W.: *Character Analysis* (1933). New York: Farrar, Straus and Giroux, 1949.

Sullivan, H.: *Clinical Studies in Psychiatry* (1956). New York: W.W. Norton, 1992.

Winnicott, D.W.: *Therapeutic Consultations in Child Psychiatry*. New York: Basic Books, 1971.

Winnicott, D.W.: *The Piggle*. London: Penguin Books, 1977.

2

Forces In Shadow

Your advantage in reading this chapter could be your readiness to look for forces that are in shadow.

Patients often ask us to reduce or eliminate their anxiety and/or depression. A drug can often do that. The drug can also obscure anxiety as a signal of threat and depression as a signal of defeat. These common symptoms may be reduced, but the dynamics remain ready to come back (Malan, 1976, Gustafson, 1986).

For example, a woman had her depression reduced by sertraline (antidepressant) and her suicidal ideation seemed to disappear. This was misleading, because the bitter fights she had been having with her husband seemed to go away when he was traveling for his business. She was not really out of danger, except for the time being before the husband returned.

George Engel's famous essay on "The clinical application of the biopsychosocial model" (1980) told the revealing opposite story of a man in the cardiac care unit for a heart attack. The longer he stayed there the worse his panic. Perhaps part of his panic was about having had a heart attack. This was the biological aspect of the panic. Engel's contributions were to the aspect of his psychology and to the social aspect. His character as a business owner was to seek always to be in charge. His social context was that he had been fully in charge as the owner. That was where he belonged. Being on the cardiac care unit was the opposite place. He entered the unit regretfully and became more and more tense the longer he stayed and more and more vulnerable to another heart attack or an extension of the heart attack he had already had and thus in more and more panic.

Janus was the Roman god of the gates between a household and the public world (and he was god of many other things as well). Positioned in the gates, the two faced god looked inward to the house and outward to the public realm. From there, he could see the buildup of dangers inward and outward. In both places he could see the danger of non-linear catastrophes erupting. Much later, of course, George Engel was performing a similar role as an astute doctor.

One of my patients found herself with a new kind of force in the world. Automatic systems for ordering things often go wrong. She felt very discouraged by one order after another going wrong. She went south for a break from our harsh winter and found herself in chilly fog. Her bank did not pay her bills for a week costing her a lot of money. Her airline ticket to go abroad would cost $700 more! As Kurt Vonnegut would say, "So it goes." We all need to be ready for electronic orders. They may work and they may not.

Another of my patients had a boyfriend who thought only of himself. He pronounced on everything without asking her feeling or thought. This is what guys tend to do? Not always! I always ask my wife to go first with her dream night. It is very much in my interest to see where she is coming from before I tell her where I am coming from. This is how equality works. There is no other way to make equality work that I know of.

I had a dream about what Jung called the shadow side. I dreamed I was interviewing patients for group therapy as I did in 1974. At that time I interviewed candidates for less than a half hour to decide whether to include them or not. Now I would never do that. I would assume that 1st impressions told me very little. I would insist on 2nd meetings with candidates to have some kind of 2nd impression. Shadows can be very powerful. I would want to sight them. I would not want an intersection with Mr. Hyde to occur in the group.

I know my own shadow. I know I am not above imagining homicide. I have never come close. There have been patients I felt like throwing through the wall. I know when it is time to usher such patients out of my office. I know that my capacity for restraint is not infinite.

These are forces likely to be hidden. I think it was Socrates who said, "Know thy self!" Most people know very little about themselves. They would rather not know. They would rather rush around being busy and smile at other people. Jung called this the persona. The 2nd impression from dreams is extremely unlikely for them.

Why is this the rule of the commonplace? I think it is the rule because it would be very painful to know oneself. Hazlitt wrote that Shakespeare had the capacity to imagine being any one of his characters in his dramas. This is what made his characters so vivid. He became them. He prided himself in carrying these things off. Most people would be scared to death to imagine being some other people. So these forces are very likely to remain hidden because these forces would be too painful and terrifying.

Sunday to Monday dreams are difficult for doctors, but perhaps for most everyone. Forces in shadow can be very unpleasant. Taking me back to camping on the Black Canyon of the Gunnison River with my older daughter, I had such a dream about a mountain lion. About midnight, I awoke to the scream of a mountain lion directly across the river perhaps thirty yards across.

Needless to say, I was terrified. All alone in this stretch of the river, in pitch dark, I felt we were defenseless if the mountain lion came across taking us for his late supper. He did not cross. He could have.

To be happening just then, this past had to be an analogy for now. It was. The analogy was for killer details. Sunday into Monday, what killer details would show up? About a patient I had only seen once, I recalled from the previous week that a primary care doctor sent me a message about this patient that her sodium was low. She wanted me to guide her about the patient taking sixty milligrams of fluoxetine (Prozac).

Not difficult for me, I could advise reducing the dose to forty milligrams a day and then get another sodium level. Low sodium can kill people. On the other hand, correcting the sodium level too fast is also dangerous. Therefore, I advised a small reduction of fluoxetine, the culprit, pretty likely.

Starting a week of practice, I can never know what killer details will show up, like the scream of a mountain lion in pitch dark. Most of what I get is quite banal, but I never know when a killer detail will be mine to take care of. This readiness is an art. It helps that I will have time with 1st impressions. I will wait for my 2nd impression if something strange has appeared, like the night I waited after the scream of the mountain lion. Nothing further happened, thankfully.

Much more common are what Sullivan (1956) called security operations. The operation makes the operator feel secure, but he or she is not more secure, actually less. For example, blaming everyone else but him or herself. Badly it will go. Another is a huge pile up of information. Another is being hysterical. Another is blaming the prescription for his or her attacking other people violently. As Sullivan would say, the operator has selective inattention for his or her move going to go badly for him or her.

Here comes a huge problem of focus that tends to hide catastrophic forces! There is such a thing as short-sightedness and long-sightedness. Bateson (1979) wrote that all vision is double description. Because one eye tends to be at a slightly different distance from the other eye in looking outward the result is a reading of depth or makes depth perception possible.

In other words it is possible to derive advantages from both short-sightedness and long-sightedness. There are things right in front of your nose you had better see and act upon at once. Like about to being kicked in the face. On the other hand only long-sightedness can be ready for things that take a long time to arrive.

References

Bateson, G.: *Mind and Nature, A Necessary Unity*. New York: Dutton, 1979.

Engel, G.: The clinical application of the biopsychosocial model. *American Journal of Psychiatry* 1980; 137 (5): 535–544.

Gustafson, J.: *The Complex Secret of Brief Psychotherapy*. New York: W.W. Norton, 1986.

Malan, D.: *The Frontier of Brief Psychotherapy*. New York: Plenum, 1976.

Sullivan, H.: *Clinical Studies in Psychiatry* (1956). New York: W.W. Norton, 1992.

3
Dilemmas

Your advantage in reading this chapter could be your readiness for dilemmas. Put simply, you can be in trouble one way, but doing the opposite puts you in trouble also, maybe far worse. For instance, most people get tired of their jobs as they get older, because all they have done is worked so they think of retirement. Not having a place in a theatre can leave you nowhere and quite lost with something that has its own difficulties.

Unbearable situations crop up commonly as in lack of company and in lack of money. These situations commonly bring on panic. Dilemmas have two horns, both bad. One horn is the present situation. The other horn is making a jump to something that might be worse. Yet it is good we could be wrong in our estimate. The dilemma is the basic structure of life (Gary Simoneau, personal communication).

For example, a medical student felt she had to be "plugged in" to her pager and cell phone and email in case something was demanded of her. Thus, she was continuously on call and continuously tense.

Even worse, she was losing herself, her identity, by this subordination. Equally worse was the move to get "unplugged" to recover herself, her identity. A catastrophe to her career seemed to be the price to recovering her identity.

Of course, some balance might be found between being "plugged in" and being "unplugged." Every doctor has to find this balance to last very long, or he or she will get ill.

Kenneth Koch published a poem in 2004 called "One train may hide another" that complicates the problems of dilemmas. Koch pictures hiking in Kenya and coming up to railroad tracks preceded by a big yellow sign saying, "Watch out for the second train!" The sign meant that you could check out the first track for danger and think yourself out of danger when the first track was clear of trains. This might set you up to get hit from the opposite direction on the second track.

In three pages, Koch presents this as an analogy for just about everything in life where you choose, as you choose a girlfriend, only to find out later that her sister was much more to your liking. Every choice hides, potentially, something better. You are then the likely loser when you choose anything!

Many patients appear to be capable of being helped. Some are. Some are not. It is best to wait to see what is going on. Sometimes patients have made such wrecks of their lives that they are far downstream in time in a relentless current (Mike Wood, personal communication). This is such bad news. We cannot tell them this. It is too painful.

It is better not to tell them this. In fact, it is too dangerous to tell them the truth. The truth can precipitate a suicide. So we just do something, like raising the dose of their medicines or referring to electroconvulsive therapy (ECT).

We might even be wrong in our estimate. Sometimes we are surprised that they actually turn things around. It is best not to play God. There may be more potential than we have thought.

I had such a patient. She had been married to a man twenty years older than her. The husband died on a vacation of a heart attack. He had taken very poor care of himself. She came to me five years later. She had been given anti-depressants that lessened her depression but she remained in apathy.

She was obviously still in grief. She felt anger at her husband and sadness and guilt that she might have taken better care of him. She shivered with these strong emotions as we talked.

What came to my mind spontaneously was Freud's essay on "Mourning and melancholia" (1917). I decided to tell her my intuition that her case was that of melancholia that could grip a person forever as it had for five years. I told her that the loss could be denied by becoming that person.

She was startled. She pointed to the jacket next to her on the couch. She said that she indeed had become him, jacket and all. Like him she was taking very poor care of herself. She was allowing her diabetes to run out of control.

Now, thoughtfully, she pivoted and made a decision that would turn things around. She told me that her neglect of herself would put a heavy burden on their son. That she refused to do! She was going to take good care of her illness. She was becoming more her own person and less like her dead husband.

Her potential shone after seeming to be dead for five years.

Sullivan (1956) was very clear that patients were often confused about what is possible and what is not possible. For example, I had a patient who broke up with his girlfriend in high school because she was so violent. Much later he found out that she never recovered from the breakup and was drinking herself to death.

He was very clear that he had had to break up with her. On the other hand he felt very guilty that he had left her to this terrible fate. In other words, he was in a very difficult dilemma, to save himself from violence or to save her from heartbreak. He was on the horns of a dilemma. Our talk about it allowed him to save himself first and bear the guilt of not saving her. He left our talk no longer confused.

You can leave a love behind and still feel love for her. You can care about a colleague and yet keep distance from her because she floods everyone with way too much information. Who said that life was going to be easy?

I had a nightmare at 4 AM. Referred by an old colleague, I had seen a patient twice. In a foreign country she had had a manic psychotic break and ended up in a psychiatric hospital. It seemed that a violent boyfriend had precipitated the break. Already on an anti-psychotic, she had come to me.

She seemed over the painful break. I weaned her off the anti-psychotic. Alas, she was not over it. She became psychotic again. I put her back on the anti-psychotic.

All was not well again. Her mother called to say she was smoking marijuana all day and night and watching television. The mother insisted that I do something about it. I must have a remedy for this stall. I asked my nurse to call the mother that I did not have a remedy.

The next thing I knew the mother called again to say that her daughter had attacked her. The police were called and came and the daughter went to jail for a couple days. Perhaps what had happened in the foreign country was similar? Maybe she had been the attacker.

Reader, you can imagine why I had a nightmare at 4 AM. Everything about the case was going rotten. What could I expect after daybreak? Michael White in Australia used to call this problem-saturation. Nothing but trouble!

D.W. Winnicott (1971) had a patient like this he called Mrs. X. It seemed that her entire life had been rotten. Her dreams were nightmares about rotten food being between her and her mother. Coming to the end of the hour's consultation, Winnicott exclaimed: "I do not see how you could bear this." The patient got out her birth certificate to show Winnicott. The patient also remembered something good, a cereal called "pobs." They had reached to something good in her after all.

Remembering all of this, I got out of my ego chill, because I saw what I would offer this patient. To remember some good in her, we would attempt together. Maybe we would find something good in her. Maybe we would not find something good in her. I was able to fall asleep.

I had learned something about myself. I can be ready for cases of problem-saturation. I can look for something good in the patients that could be defended. This is what Winnicott called a lifeline. Some things are about life and death. The focus is about engaging extreme forces, for ill or for good. As Winnicott would also say, this is the challenge of the case.

The unconscious loves what is beautiful that can be defended. Many beautiful things cannot be and are not defended. Beautiful on 1st impression often is not beautiful on 2nd impression. It is important to wait. The pivotal action is psychotherapy.

You deserve more from me about how I see a huge host of patients that are not going anywhere. Stevenson (1886) taught me how this dynamism works to make what he called downward going men (and women). I notice that they are banged about in countless ways. Yes, I mean banged about. It can be literal smashing as in accidents. It can be cruel relationships. It can be meaningless jobs. It can be jobs that overwhelm anyone who takes them. Often there is no alternative as for Dr. Jeykll.

What happens? Will it be drift into despair? Will it be eruption of rage like that of Mr. Hyde? Diversions like gambling and drinking and drugs? We often can do little but prescribe heavy sedation.

Why do I see an advantage in such a dire picture? To alert you to save yourself! You might do the little that can be done and then move on. I certainly do not want you to become a Dr. Jeykll yourself! That is only being nice and letting people walk all over him or you.

After writing that paragraph, later that afternoon in clinic, I noticed that patients could get an advantage in frankly recognizing impossible people, as in those who can never stop intruding if given any opening at all.

You can think about this for yourself. There are plenty of other ways people can be impossible if you let then have any opening at all. Immediately, I thought of my patient who screeches at a fast rate. I do her the favor of asking her to be quiet. This takes a few minutes.

I have another patient who attempts to conduct every thing that enters my mind. In opening sentences, she tells me what I must not think. I have learned to look away from her steely gaze and movements of a conductor.

Now that I have opened this subject, I realize it has a vast domain. You can think of nearly everyone you know who has figures of speech and gestures you find unbearable. So stay away from them as best you can! Or keep things brief!

References

Freud, S.: Mourning and melancholia. *The Standard Edition of the Complete Psychological Works of Sigmund Freud* (1917), Volume 14, pp. 237–258. London: Hogarth Press, 1953.

Koch, K.: *One Train*. New York: Alfred A. Knopf, 2004.

Stevenson, R.: *The Strange Case of Dr. Jekyll and Mr. Hyde* (1886). New York: Puffin Books, 1985.

Sullivan, H.: *Clinical Studies in Psychiatry* (1956). New York: W.W. Norton, 1992.

Winnicott, D.W.: *Therapeutic Consultations in Child Psychiatry*. New York: Basic Books, 1971.

Reversals

Chapter 4   Life Lies

Chapter 5   Will Trying To Do The Work Of The Imagination

Chapter 6   Double Takes

4 Life Lies

Your advantage in reading this chapter could be your readiness for attractive things that turn out to be dangerous. Attractive things can reverse and go afoul. Ibsen called them life lies (Goldman, 1999).

That was also Aristotle's plot of tragedy. Sophocles' *Oedipus Rex* is the most famous example. Oedipus unwittingly killed his father for barging Oedipus off the road on the way to Thebes. When Oedipus got to Thebes, he unwittingly married his mother. These two moves were attractive but turned out to be tragic when Oedipus discovered what he had done.

As I explained in the last chapter, one dilemma can hide another, but it is also true that one part can hide another (Koch, 2004)

Thomas Hardy's short story, *On The Western Circuit* (1894), illustrated a similar reversal. A young attorney comes to a small town the night before he is to appear in circuit court. Darkness is falling and the little town is having a kind of carnival. A merry-go-round is in action with plenty of noise. Standing and looking at it, the young attorney catches sight of a beautiful young woman in red velvet going up and own on her horse. Her beautiful smile meets his every time she comes around.

Hardy's long single sentence summarizes what is about to happen that is not a good thing:

Each time she approached the half of her orbit that lay nearest him they gazed at each other with smiles, and with that unmistakable expression which means so little at the moment, yet so often leads up to passion, heart-ache, union, disunion, devotion, overpopulation, drudgery, discontent, resignation, despair.

The three examples of the part hiding the whole situation that will become reversals, from Sophocles, Koch and Hardy, seem to me now very much like dreams. Indeed, I have been thinking about how dreams could anticipate probable reversals at least as early as in my Myerson Lecture in 1987. The first I called *The Transported Daughter*. The second I called *The Orange Seaplane*. The third I called *The Man in His Fort*. All three are clear examples of how a patient might be woken up to how she or he is unwittingly headed for danger. With the dream in hand it might not be too late or it might be too late. Life lies (Goldman, 1999) can go on for a lifetime. Let us look at them, one at a time.

First, consider this reversal of the transported daughter: In session eighty-three, she presented "a little clip" of a dream, of being in a small plane, where she could watch the pilot up ahead of her, easing down into a beautiful, dark, green, leafy woods, which reminded her of walks with her father as a child. The amazing aspect was that there was no fear in the descent, but a gliding like a bird. The lurch came at the end of the hour, when she was obliged to come out of this reverie, onto the hard, cold surface of going back into the world. The stress fell there, I suggested. She could draw on the remembrance of a loving relationship with her father, but then the fall from this grace made her cry out, it hit so hard and suddenly.

Second, consider The Orange Seaplane: Listen to how metaphor carries a sudden, enormous distance for another patient of mine, a woman I was just getting to know. Allow me to say only that I knew already that she had felt unwanted as a child and that much of her fantasy about escaping the farm was to become a hostess of a game show. In her tenth session, she related the following dream. She was on the ground. It was in trouble.

She heard a plane overhead. The CB radio said it crashed immediately. She felt glad she was on the ground.

Her associations to being on the ground came to what she called "an average, basic, regulation picnic," which was boring. Her associations to the plane suddenly put before us "an orange seaplane" (which was giving rides) she had once seen on a lake in Northern Wisconsin. Finally, most extraordinary, the orange seaplane "fell straight down like rain." When I asked her to let her mind go with the falling straight down like rain, she became very frightened saying that she didn't know where that would lead. I told her I understood that she could feel I would not protect her. I recalled her having begun the hour talking about fear of losing control to me, her remembering trying to talk to her father as a child, until one day he yelled at her to shut up because he was watching television. That was the last chance she ever gave him to listen to her. I said to her that she puts men in control, but she cannot follow them because they do not look out for her.

At this point, she began to cry quietly, saying, "It's too painful. No one ever has."

The dream was to have a very big effect on a very practical matter. The following, eleventh session, two weeks later, she told me she was tempted to borrow a huge sum of money to buy a business from a charming, exciting man who was pressing her hard to take it on. I suspected a disaster in the making, worse than the four disappointments of love with four charming men in the last two years, all of which had crashed, for this would not only hurt but throw her deeply into debt. I told her that I could understand her wanting the thrill of the ride, which would get her out of the "average, basic, regulation picnic" of her dull, boring life, but that I could not tell if this orange seaplane was put together badly, so-so, or well, and that I doubted that she could tell either.

The metaphor let us get back and forth between her dullness and her taking an exciting ride, however foolish. Then, for the first time in her life, she told me in the twelfth session, she actually turned down the ride, after consulting with several business friends. Now she was very sad. One final turn, which some of you have already anticipated? In the twelfth session, she entrusted me with a very terrifying dream, which explained why she had been so desperate to jump on any orange seaplane that came on her lake. The gist of it was that she was visiting her parents' home, where a crowd was gathered as for a wake. Her aunt showed her a burglar and fire alarm system in a special room, which seemed to make some sense, until she went upstairs, becoming suddenly aware that it was all stone up there and that there was no room for herself. Her sister was terrified for her, but wouldn't tell her what for. A certain uncle who was kind might explain, but the family wouldn't let her near him. Then she had the terrifying thought herself, "I am the fire, for which they have the alarms." My following the great sudden distance carried by one metaphor has aroused enough trust to allow her to give me· one even more unbearable.

Third, consider The Man in His Fort: Often times the very surface of the hour, its manifest content, so to speak, will show where the turn or drop or reversal falls. In the Case of the Man in His Fort, the patient's dream in the thirty-first session was as follows: He is moving into a house which has one bedroom upstairs, which is connected by a strange passageway to the downstairs, where lives his father who is guarding the place. He goes downstairs to receive a delivery and begins rising, unable to stop. His associations to the bedroom connected by the slanting strange passageway are to the famous fortress of Cartagena in South America he once visited, "very defendable in an ingenious way since the passage magnified the sound of possible assailants." This arrangement reminded him of being over-weight, which he feels makes him invisible so that he overhears indiscretions in his presence. His thought about his father is that he is less and less willing to bow to him. His rising reminds him of a period of sexual exploration in college in which he felt alive "head to toe," which led his father to denounce him as "immoral."

Now telling this, he begins to cry admitting, "He was right, I cared more about sex than anything." I say, "Yes, but your dad mistook this part of you for everything." He replies that the house in the dream is the new one he bought with his girlfriend, which he very much wants to hold onto, fearing to lose the house and her if he allows himself to feel his hunger for being fully alive. I say I understand both, that he wants to be fully alive and he wants to keep his house, his security. He is enormously relieved. This reversal is well marked. I do not have much difficulty so long as I put the stress on the "rising, unable to stop." The distance traversed by the metaphor, from the Cartagena fortress to the rising out in the open, finds this individual in his preoccupation, which brings out and goes over the most unbearable fall in his life, being denounced and disowned by his father.

All three of these patients seemed to have something attractive, but this part falsified the whole situation. The attractive part fell apart, literally, in a complete reversal of fate. It was not sound.

Now thirty years later we will see how performing a myth of being a hero could be foreseen for its collapse. A young man had a pretty girlfriend the summer before each went separate ways to college. By the following spring he learned that his girlfriend had replaced him with an older man who was very rich. The young man completely fell apart, losing sixty pounds and being unable to continue his schooling.

I saw him in consultation to one of our residents for one hour. He had had an exceedingly dramatic dream in three parts that would clarify the forces that explained his fall. In the first part of the dream, he woke up in the dark and imagined that the circuit breaker was thrown. As he put it, his power was out. He went downstairs and turned off the circuit breaker. As he turned around he found himself face to face with a beautiful girl with nothing on but her panties. His power was back in.

In the second part of the dream he was lying in his own bed as when he was eight years old. He heard steps coming up on the staircase. Next he knew this robber was standing over him. He was both the robber and the victim. As the robber his power was in. As the victim his power was completely gone.

In the third part of the dream he went down the hall as his present self to the bathroom. He found himself face to face with the beautiful girl again.

As we talked about his being the victim at eight years old, he remembered that a robbery of the house had occurred at that time. It had been quite terrifying.

I said to him that the dream called out the importance of his childhood vulnerability. He replied that he never could accept losing at anything. As early as kindergarten he picked fights every day and ended up in the principal's office. He had also been something of a vandal.

I told him that children who turn antisocial like this had been wronged. He thought I said wrong. No, I meant wronged. Children wronged turn to wronging others. Like Malcolm X whose father was murdered when Malcolm was five years old. At first he was stealing grapefruits. Later he became a violent burglar with a gun.

He could not think of how he had been wronged? He had lived with good grandparents until he was six. Why? Because his mother had concocted a business even before he was born and with his father had worked day and night for six years to make the business go.

So I said this could explain how he felt abandoned? He shook his head and said I was trying to put this into his head. He crouched forward in a menacing way towards me.

I knew I had better back off! My power was in and his power was out. He simply had to be the one with power. As in his triptych dream, he had to be on top. His was a very vulnerable power. He would quickly attack to reinstate himself. This part he had to play was of being hero in a myth. The mythical part was incredibly vulnerable to being reversed.

Several years later he was admitted to our inpatient service for psychosis triggered in part by heavy drug use. He acted like a king on the service, insulting all of the staff continually. His myth would let him do nothing else.

Far worse was what happened to the Notre Dame de Paris. The idea was to repair the wooden roof and spire. Instead it caught fire from the work and destroyed most of the cathedral. The thing to be improved destroyed most of its beautiful context.

The idea seemed attractive evidently. Our species seems to be extremely vulnerable to this tragic kind of mistake. I haven't said much in this book about sexual attraction. This part of a sexual attraction as 1st impression makes for a very dangerous narrow focus that cannot see the 2nd impression that disastrous life that may go with it. The part falsifies the whole situation. Freud called it wish fulfillment as illusion or even as delusion. Ibsen called it a life lie.

Marx (1867) called it commodity fetishism. The thing bought will give you a great life. Almost everything sold on television works by this illusion. You probably have noticed that the smiling actors are made to look stupid. No matter! I suppose this conveys that any buyer, however lacking in judgment, will benefit hugely by purchase of the thing.

Voting mostly works by the same mechanism of selling. Buy this candidate and everything will be taken care of beautifully. Not so! The image or the phrase seems to be sufficient to capture the nod.

References

Goldman, M.: *Ibsen, The Dramaturgy Of Fear*. New York: Columbia University Press, 1999.

Hardy, T.: *On the Western Circuit. Life's Little Ironies*. Penguin, London, 1894.

Koch, K.: *One Train*. New York: Alfred A. Knopf, 2004.

Marx, K.: *Capital, Critique of Political Economy* (in German). Verlag von Otto Meisner, Hamburg, 1867.

5

Will Trying To Do The Work Of The Imagination

Your advantage in reading this chapter could be your readiness for willfulness that will be big trouble for you. Willfulness is a kind of thing that destroys its context. Things are supposed to work anywhere. Yes, hammers work in a lot of places. But they get you in trouble in other places.

It is easy to push ahead without knowing where you are going. The results are likely to be poor. Yeats (Tate, 1934, p. 176) called this the definition of rhetoric or the art of persuasion. So much of advertising and business and politics take this form.

The work of the imagination is to map out the territory you would like to explore in advance. You are far more likely to find your way.

Binswanger (1963) gave us a very important example of will gone wrong in his essay called Verstiegenheit (Extravagance in translation). The Binswanger family had the Bellevue Sanatorium in Kreuzlingen not far from the Alps for several generations. They were very familiar with mountain climbers that got themselves in big trouble. The climbers got up high with no way to get down. They had just pushed ahead.

A familiar example from the Ivy League graduates is to get hired on Wall Street to make a lot of money by working eighteen-hour days. It is a set up for exhaustion and losing yourself. It is a good way to get run over on your bicycle. You did not see it coming. Once you stop, you may never be willing to go back to these shelves of prestige. You may not know what to do at all. This is Verstiegenheit, of will trying to do the work of the imagination.

Another familiar example from older people is to work forty years and retire, only to find that having no stage is deadly. You might not live much longer, doing nothing. I had a dream about such a man whose wife was leaving him and his business finished. I had a nightmare of a big green striped bus rocketing down the steep hill right at me. I was supposed to tackle it. Then the US Army was cornering me and hanging me. I often dream the plight of my patients. My nightmare put me in the deadly end of the patient. My colleagues seem to think you can buck up mood in such men with ECT and then he would have a life. As my nightmare stressed, so forcefully, this man was finished. My colleagues have a certain extravagance about saving people.

Another patient had a dream about nearly everyone being swamped by too much detail. Nevertheless, they talked non-stop. This will concealed the emptiness, like an empty New Yorker shopping bag with nothing in it, a very prestigious monolog. It usurps the work of imagination about having something worthwhile to do and thus something worthwhile to say.

It is like spending billions of dollars on building a nearly two thousand-mile wall between the United States and Mexico. This wilful fiction is what comes out of the mouth of a so-called President. He insists this is a national emergency. The work of the imagination would be to understand all the emergencies this country actually is vulnerable to.

There are very many. This situation reminds me of a certain director of national security, Donald Rumsfeld who resigned. His very brief press conference was the only thing he ever said that made sense.

There are known knowns. These are things we know that we know. There are known unknowns. That is to say, there are things that we know we don't know. But there are also unknown unknowns. There are things we don't know we don't know.

In other words, if you cannot imagine certain dangers, you are helpless to defend yourself from them. You will national security and do not have it. Your talk is just rhetoric. This is much of politics and advertising and business. You can sell fiction. It passes for knowledge.

As Sullivan (1956) said, security operations, like those of Rumsfeld and Trump, can make people feel secure when they are not.

I had a dream about this will. I dreamed that I was an electrician asked to fix something in three houses with the help of two students. The students were eager to prop open the manhole covers to start to do something on the electrical systems of these houses. As for me I had no idea of what these homeowners wanted and I had no knowledge of electrical equipment.

This was will plunging ahead with no idea of what the homeowners needed. It is typical top-down action with no sensitivity for what is needed from the bottom-up. This is analogous to the action of Trumpistan.

No doubt also that it is the action of top-down psychiatry on treatment resistant depression. When anti-depressant drugs do not work, the treatment becomes an electrical job consisting of ECT (electroconvulsant therapy), TMS (transmagnetic stimulation) or ketamine infusions. The treatment needs to know nothing of the dynamics of defeat in depression. Like the two students in my dream the treatment just plunges ahead. It has plenty of momentum and further acceleration.

Not me. Curiously I felt so relaxed in the clinic after my dream night. I did no more than I wanted. I had no interest in being an electrician doing things to miserable people. My interest was listening to the stories of the patients. I cared about listening accurately to these patients while watching for their non-verbal signals to punctuate the message with their bodies. I love working very slowly, doing the work of imagination quite as Yeats (Tate, 1934) did, Yeats the poet.

Sunday to Monday nights bring about a prospective dream on the week about to dawn. Often two prospectives! If the earlier dream in the night is dire, the later dream in the night is beautiful, and vice versa. If the first is about death, the second is about life.

For example I had an early night dream of a rule that deprived a person of what little he once had. That is what Dr. Jekyll did by exhausting himself in taking care of others. This is what Stevenson (1886) called downward going men. Utterson the lawyer made friends with such. I? No. However, I am obliged to see death setting in as a doctor. I have to endure it. It gives me a cold chill, even as I write this. Would I be able to go back to sleep?

Yes, I was able to go back to sleep. Before dawn, I dreamed of a party for children and adults. This party got out of hand in its pleasures. Then I drew pictures for the children of what they had imagined. This got them further out of hand with our first year residents and the police! There can be such a thing as too much life late in the night after too much death early in the night.

What is the advantage of imagining these extremes of life and death? It reminds us that we cannot will what we are going to see in the patients. They can be moving anywhere between these extremes and some move in quite a mixed-up fashion. Their energy is theirs. My energy is to read where they are going.

In other words, the pair of opposite dreams works as a 2nd impression on the range of possibilities I am going to come across. From it I am more apt to be ready.

In the following night, I got a very different lesson from a trio of dreams. Catching ten trout, I divided them into two trout for five suppers. This is impossible! I never catch ten trout around here. Making grandstand basketball shots in a nearby park was the second impossible dream. Our car jerked around in the snow was the third impossible dream. I managed to wrestle the car from falling into a deep hole and turn the car on its side to pass through a narrow gap. Such antics reminded me of a Charlie Chaplin movie.

Extravagance was my lesson. Heroic will usurped the place of imagining that is accurate. I wanted no part of such a farce. This kind of heroic doctor was not for me. It was fiction. I have had plenty of patients who demand such miraculous performances from their doctor. I decline it.

I wanted no part of this either as an athlete. Athletes get nowhere on farce and fiction. Going to work with my tennis coach, I knew he would show me what was not quite right about my strokes. He would imitate how my strokes looked to him. Then I would ask him how he performed these strokes. At once the differences were obvious to me. This is the work of the imagination that is accurate. Will is a very poor substitute. In fact, it is no substitute at all.

I had a young man as a patient who had a nightmare about his will and lack of imagination. Knowing nothing about sex, having never had it, and never come into its power, this was his nightmare. Hardly noting she looked strange, on 1st impression, he took her to bed. Then he drove her back to her father's house that was perched on the edge of a cliff and had a big porch over an abyss. In being introduced to the father, he was shocked to notice that he only had a white shirt down to his knees. The 2nd impression that would give him a picture of the context for his first sexual experience was beginning to unfold. Now meeting the father he could not help noticing the father was a creep. Now he knocked over the father's wine glasses and he found he had no money in his wallet to pay for them. He woke up flushed and chilled. Hopefully, it is not too late for him to wake up.

Here is a very different kind of will, namely my own. Having a house for over forty years can fill it up with too many materials that are not needed. Sneaks up on you? It seems so.

In my study I have had the habit of tacking papers to my white walls. For one reason or another I liked them. I did not imagine that such a big accumulation would get in my way. It was too much.

So one day I began to take down the papers. I was astonished by the layers I no longer needed. In particular one caught my attention that I could find helpful. It was a page (p. 361) from Daisetz Suzuki on *Zen and Japanese Culture* (1939). It said that nature was always in motion. It said that being in motion could be beautiful. It said that the static was death itself.

So I worked hard to get my decks clear of the static that could only get in my way. Little did I imagine that I would have a nightmare about it at midnight! It was about my attempting to get rid of evil people. The more I tried to get rid of them the more of them surrounded me.

So I went up to my study to keep from waking up my wife. This was far worse. I felt surrounded by the tacks no longer hidden by papers. I started to take down the tacks I could pull up easily like dandelions. There were far too many of them, so I stopped and I went back to bed.

I did not know if I would be awake all night? Once I stopped willing to clear my decks, I fell asleep. I was very surprised to have a beautiful dream. I dreamed I was back in medical school taking a summer scholarship in 1965 at the Royal Edinburgh Hospital. To my good fortune I got to go to a lecture by R.D. Laing and talk with him.

In my beautiful dream I was going with Laing on a two-week bicycle ride and seminar in England, very mathematical and very musical. This seemed to be happening on a beautiful orange red tablet. My balance was being reestablished. If I chose to take one thing in, I would get rid of one thing I do not need.

In other words, I could remove my tacks slowly. Otherwise I would lose my balance. I felt at peace. But the nightmare came back as I was waking up in the morning. We were going into an acrid fire in a medical hospital. This was not a good idea. The flush chill comes back, signaling I was attempting too much, too fast, too many words on a page, too much of everything. 2nd impressions can save us.

A vast number of patients are going too fast. All they see is 1st impressions. They are short-sighted. Because they are only will, a kind of will made out of titanium, they are intractable.

Sullivan (1956) called this inflexible will a "security operation." If it comes in many shapes, they all bestow a feeling of security that makes the person actually less secure.

You can see it in crowds of adolescents (Mike Wood, personal communication). They tend to be present only in the moment and not in the past or the future. Must there not be a big advantage to this presentness with the group? Yes, the feeling of belonging. You can see the delight on their faces and hear their uproarious laughter. They feel important. They feel confident.

Adolescents who cannot join this cacophony tend to lose confidence (Gilligan, 1982). The fortunate exceptions are those with considerable backing from their parents or teachers or mentors. Thus they can see in original ways and hold to them.

Beyond high school in college or professional schools, some of them can have an astounding confidence in their own short-sightedness. I remember it in myself. I had a big old Ford Fairlane from my father the Ford dealer. I used it chiefly to play in tennis tournaments around New England in the summers. Suddenly, my big old car clunked and refused to go backwards. Was I daunted? Not in the least!

I just arranged to go forward only. I managed to position my car so I never needed to go backwards. I got away with it. At the end of the summer, I drove the car from Boston back to Michigan across Ontario. An Ontario policeman stopped me for my lack of an outer rear view mirror. It never occurred to him to have me go backwards. I just promised the policeman I would take care of replacing the rear view mirror when I got home. What hubris! A Greek word for excessive self-confidence! I was totally in the present with no reference to the past or the future. I was all short-sightedness with no capacity for long-sightedness. If I had had long-sightedness I would have been able to think of some other way to replace this car that had only a one-direction transmission. Anything else was plumb dangerous!

Yes, I am implying that adolescence and early adulthood tend to be ruled by intractable will. Some never get any farther. This takes many forms.

I am not sure of what form of intractable will is most common. I am most familiar with the security operation of the increase pack (Canetti, 1984) because I have been surrounded by it all my life. It is the intractable will to increase numbers, numbers of anything! My grandfather David, a minister and later a Professor at Carnegie Tech, kept track of his numbers of sermons, choir rehearsals, weddings and funerals and I forget what else every week.

His older son, my father, kept track of Fords and used cars sold, whether he made money on them or not. Mostly not much because Ford Motor Company squeezed him to turn over his supply of cars so Ford could make the money. He was a page out of Arthur Miller's 1949 famous play, Death of A Salesman.

His younger son, my uncle, was Chief Photographer of the *Saginaw News*. I knew him best as one of Navy photographers who photographed the Japanese attack on Pearl Harbor. I studied them countless times as a young boy. That seemed to me a great thing. Back in Saginaw he was in continuous demand to take photographs for the *News* of just about everything. That also impressed me.

Some other heroics of numbers were a continual preoccupation for me as a young boy from baseball cards that came with Bubble Gum. The picture of a given player was on the front of a card and his numbers elaborated beyond belief, like batting average, slugging average, home runs, triples, doubles, errors and I forget what else. My head was jammed with these numbers. That is the point.

I was taught to get perfect numbers myself. I was extremely good at it. In elementary school, you got S for satisfactory and U for unsatisfactory. I got only one U, all the rest Ss. Even that single U made me indignant. Rosy Writer, my second grade teacher, gave the entire class a U for "uses time well," because the class was in an uproar when she was out of the classroom. As for junior and senior high, all As.

You get the point. Numbers rule our heads. The bigger the number the better you are and the smaller number the more worthless you are. I need not elaborate. I am not the only one ruled by this. You have been too. You too have had an intractable fascination with numbers. I had a patient with the worst case of it. She was always told as a child that she was worthless. For the next sixty years, she had to prove continually that she knew great friends and had great opinions. Nothing she touched was lacking in greatness. Needless to elaborate, everyone wanted to run away from her as quickly as possible.

Addicts are intractable about getting "my drug." Doctors cannot bear them. Doctors themselves have to keep up their numbers and their documentations. Assistant professors have to amass papers published to get tenure. Each paper is given a number for the "impact" of the journal published in. Of course, first person authorship counts and second and third and fourth are relatively valueless. Once established in tenure as an associate professor, keeping up your numbers is an incessant worry.

Politics is a similar worry as the numbers rise or fall every day as in the current struggle for being the Democratic candidate for President. God, help us, we pray, to care less and less about this and more and more about something beautiful and moving and profound. Such would be a bottom-up view of this top-down world of ratings. This top-down world is one of continuous anxiety. It is one of intractable will with no imagination. In psychiatry, imagination seems not to be important at all. I beg to disagree.

My wife Ruth pointed out to me that Dante regarded his Inferno as a perpetual place for intransigent and intractable people to be punished forever. They won't give and neither will the punishment. His guide Virgil had to warn Dante over and over again not to linger for but a brief exchange or he would swoon. Indeed he did pass out several times and Virgil had to pull him out of danger to move on.

You too had better not linger over my cases in this my chapter. They are dangerous for you. Move on! I think I will take a nap.

Do we have in English a word called a "life lie"? No, but Ibsen (Goldman, 1999) had such an idea in Norwegian and in all his tragic plots. The plots are all about will climbing too high, a failure of imagination, and then to come crashing down from extravagant heights, like the so-called master builder. Some builder! A more common example would be total self-sacrifice expecting to be requited by the harsh spouse. It is not so.

Is there something analogous in everyday life? Yes, it is a failure to judge one's life all along, and then to see too late that it was spent poorly. The intractable will was spent badly. It was profoundly inaccurate in its lack of imagination and thus in its judgment.

References

Binswanger, L.: *Extravagance in Being-In-The World*. New York: Harper and Row, 1963.

Canetti, E.: *Crowds and Power*. New York: Farrar, Straus and Giroux, 1984.

Gilligan, C.: *In a Different Voice: Psychological Theory and Women's Development*. Cambridge, Massachusetts: Harvard University Press, 1982.

Goldman, M.: *Ibsen, The Dramaturgy of Fear*. New York: Columbia University Press, 1999.

Miller, A.: *Death of a Salesman*. Harmondsworth: Penguin Books, 1996.

Stevenson, R.: *The Strange Case of Dr. Jekyll and Mr. Hyde* (1886). New York: Puffin Books, 1985.

Sullivan, H.: *Clinical Studies in Psychiatry* (1956). New York: W.W. Norton, 1992.

Suzuki, D.: *Zen and Japanese Culture*. Princeton, New Jersey: Princeton University Press, 1939.

Tate, A.: Three Types of Poetry (1934) in *Essays of Four Decades*. Wilmington, Delaware: ISI Books, 1999.

6

Double Takes

Your advantage in reading this chapter could be your readiness for a 1st impression that seems a good idea, only to be followed at once with a 2nd impression that it is a very bad idea. Immediate reversals are very common. Here is an example. I dreamed that I was being made the steward of a beautiful trout stream and a beautiful wooden house. Such a gift! At once, I saw that the house was indefensible. Already crazy people were firing up the fireplace as if they owned it. I told them to get out. Is this a good idea? Not really. They would be back in no time to burn down the house in revenge. This is a double take (Michael Hoyt, personal communication), a reversal at once that saves you from taking a dubious gift. The shadow is there to be seen, sometimes, if you are alert to it. Freud (1910) called these primal words that contain their opposite, such as sanction to approve of versus sanction to punish (Michael Hoyt, personal communication).

Romantic myths further this, such as finding your perfect double. Of course, they do not exist. Another is that of Don Quijote who attacked devils on the dusty plain of Spain. Of course, these devils were quite ordinary beings going about their business. Another romantic myth is that of loving everyone. Of course, many people are not lovable and some do not want anyone to get close to them.

Compromise becomes necessary for those who want something that can last or, as we say now, to be sustainable.

A friend of mine (Gary Simoneau, personal communication) just commented how mixed up people are, like Joyce full of clear-sightedness and mendacity.

I had a patient for a very long time, decades, who believed in pure love. That is, no selfishness. He was taken advantage of consistently. He did all the giving. He got very little back. It did him no good to discuss this with him.

Of course, there are plenty of people who believe in pure selfishness. Our so-called president seems to be so. One of the commentators of MSNBC, Joy Reid, called this Trumpistan. He seems still to have many followers like him and liking him. He seems to lie every time he speaks. This seems to be acceptable to his followers.

I do not find it acceptable. I believe that relationships that last well are all about a balance between taking and giving. Partners take turns. All the marital therapists I know to be helpful know that mediation aims towards equality. Not all the time. Rather a back and forth as needs arise in each of the partners. Each knows when he or she is taking and looks for giving back.

Another way of taking this problem is that when we are young we want pure great and beautiful worlds. They all turned out to be mixed-up. For example, I went to MIT on a National Merit Scholarship and backed by my love of Linus Pauling's book of chemistry I had been studying way ahead of my peers. MIT turned out to be all mixed-up in countless ways.

Having gone every Sunday to hear George Buttrick's sermons in Harvard Chapel, especially about the one on God being in eclipse that made so much sense to me about my troubles at MIT, I transferred to Harvard College. George Buttrick was gone. Paul Tillich's two-year course on the history of philosophy consisted only of Tillich repeating the so-called profundity of "being."

However, his section man conducted the best discussions I had ever been in. He also conducted a seminar for some of us at his house on the comedy of the Gospel of Mark. He also recited poetry with an eloquence I had never heard. I had reached the great world for the third time.

Alas, it was not to last, like the others to come. My section man got a faculty position in California when I got a residency in San Francisco. When I visited him with my new wife, I was shocked he was conducting naked parties for his students in his swimming pool.

There were many already like this for me, where a great world was mixed up with foolishness or even tragedy. I had sent the great English poet laureate, Ted Hughes, a copy of my new book, *The New Interpretation of Dreams* (1997). He sent me back his book, *Winter Pollen* (1994) with this inscription: "To a bedazzled fan of The New Interpretation of Dreams and the Daniel behind it."

I was thrilled by his recognition of what I had made, but it began a long study of his very mixed-up life of brilliance and tragedy.

I could write pages and pages upon this sequence of 1st impressions as great and beautiful, followed by 2nd impressions where beautiful and terrible were all mixed-up.

Now I can say that the great and beautiful 1st impressions gave me something that I never lost. Gun Mill Farm above the Connecticut River Valley of my college roommate, from a very mixed-up family, stayed with me and much later became our eighty acres of prairie and woods and a very beautiful cabin.

If something great and beautiful was not pure and came with many and often dangerous faults, I could still conserve its virtue. My young colleague, Stuart Jones (personal communication), said to me: "You are not just talking about 2nd impressions, but 3rd and 4th and 5th impressions."

I had three dreams in one night about this problem of the great and beautiful. First I dreamed I was going to guide a fly-fishing expedition. Then I realized I did not want to do it. I did not want to take on this burden.

Second I dreamed that a pack of teenagers next door vandalized my beautiful cedar hot (winter) or cold (summer) tub in our back yard. When I went next door to accost them, I found they had destroyed my tub altogether led by a young woman. They were monsters. As Henry Beston (1928) wrote, "Man can be less than man or more than man, and both are monsters, the last more dread (Foreword, XXXV)." I was being reminded.

Third I dreamed that it was possible to play at destroying great beauty, as performed by Shakespeare's company or the actors in the classical tragic theatre of Athens. Evidently, this has the benefit of being ready for great beauty to be brought down. I also thought of a great army disappearing into blizzards as that of Napoleon in the depths of Russia.

In a more everyday context, I thought of my tennis coach who has taught me how to sustain an attack for very long points. I also thought of sustaining attack necessary in the NCAA basketball tournament.

Finally, I was reminded of Jean Renoir who said he was happy very late in life because he was making the films he wanted to make and he had accomplices to do it. Verdi composed his requiem very late in his life. A professor of poetry at Cornell conducted poetry contests and wrote his best book at age one hundred and one.

Great beauty can be brought down. Having company in playing tragic reversals and playing comic reversals allows a long rich life.

Psychosis comes to the foreground at this point. Tragic reversal is its name. As such it is not well known. Over fifty years ago I wrote my thesis on it for my medical degree. Preceding me was William James (1901–1902).

Essentially, James had lectured and written that psychosis was a dynamic about collapse of identity, often in a religious context such as Puritan New England. Into this vacuum of identity, identification with God swelled up. For the Puritan ministers in practice, their job was to attempt to bring the God-complex into line with the congregation. Pulling this off sometimes worked.

Now more than one hundred years later, this common dynamic is hardly ever known or discussed. For example, our department had a patient who was a nothing who became Jesus Christ on the Cross, by stabbing himself over and over again. Far worse would have been to stab others.

Strangely, the religious meaning of this behavior did not get discussed at all. The collapse of identity did not get discussed. The reversal of a life did not get discussed. The grandiosity of claiming to be Jesus Christ did not get discussed.

The advantage to my readers is for them to anticipate what often happens to downward going persons. A grandiose religious claim can rush in suddenly! Downward going may be tragic. Upward going would be comic in the sense of victory over defeat. False victory might be just that, but it can take hold of a person in its grip. This is worth comprehending for my readers who might be astonished by their patients who undergo these sequences of reversal. Double takes are very fast reversals.

Another difficult yet common problem occurs when patients secretly take high doses of benzodiazepines (clonazepam, alprazolam, lorazepam and so forth) and become dependent upon them. They insist their anxiety and depression and panic attacks are unbearable without their drug of choice. A similar addiction occurs with prescribed opioids or with street drugs like marijuana and cocaine and heroin.

The doctor finds himself in a double take. First, he knows that he cannot prescribe these drugs that will get more and more out of hand. Second, he knows that he will run into heated objections if he calls for a gradual taper like the Ashton protocol with diazepam that can be prescribed at an equivalent to the addictive dose and in place of it, and then reduce it very slowly over months, by reducing it by one milligram every two weeks.

These patients act with us like they are the doctors, not us. We cannot allow them to take over. Neither can we punish them by quick tapers. The Ashton taper is the third option that can be welcomed by some patients. Some insist upon their own will. Such grandiosity is not amazing. It is commonplace.

I had not understood how fundamental turns out to be the double take reversal. The terrible fire in Notre Dame de Paris put me through it. For days, I kept seeing it. It was hard to attend to anything else.

Let us go to the double take reversal that had a strange grip on me. The April 29, 2019 cover photograph of *The New Yorker* was something I could not get rid of. The photograph is taken from the front and western approach to the cathedral. It is a dark silhouette. From behind it is the enormous orange and yellow glare of the fire itself. The sacred I have loved had been consumed by hell itself. There could be nothing worse.

I have loved the cathedrals for a very long time. I assumed they were all granite. It never occurred to me that wood eight hundred years old remained in the roofs. That is their vulnerability. I had assumed they were invulnerable, these Notre Dames. The shock of their vulnerability takes time to get over.

Everything beautiful has its vulnerability. That is the danger of being in love. Infants are born with this instinctively. They take as much milk as they desire and then they quickly turn their heads away until they want the milk back again. This oscillation has to go well. Good mothers accept it and can even laugh about it. So fierce it is! We all need to be fierce like this. It is the engine of evolution, the so-called Lotka Scenario. All mammals get to forage on milk as infants. They take what they want and need and then they push it away.

As we get older, we do something similar. We go to college imagining it will be great. Well, yes. But then it is not what we want. The other college we imagine will be the right one. That turns out not to be true either. If we are well, we pull in what is good for us and push away what is not good for us. We do it continuously when we are fully present to our senses. Otherwise we will be very confused. Contemplation means to be present to the temple. Is it what we want just now or not? Maybe yes, maybe no.

Aren't borderlines another matter? Well, yes and no. I had one who would not talk with me at all for months. Her mother just told me that her daughter took an overdose and refused to go into the hospital. So mother was stuck with her. The mother did it well. She insisted the daughter get out of bed, take showers, help out with cooking and so forth. This was probably more than a hospital could accomplish.

I did not hear from the two of them for another month or two. Suddenly, the daughter ended up in the hospital for a suicide attempt by overdose for a second time. Perhaps this was progress that the daughter went into the hospital. She was discharged the next day. Two nights later, when

I was backup to the residents in the emergency department, I was called that the patient tried to cut herself. Should we admit her or not? It seemed to be too dangerous to discharge her.

The next day the resident taking care of her on the ward called me to say they were discharging her because she would not talk about anything except to say she was no longer suicidal. She was on my outpatient schedule that very afternoon. I dreaded it.

The daughter came with her mother. Surprisingly, the daughter made no objection to my nurse sitting in on the session. I structured the meeting. I asked the mother to explain what she thought had happened. Then she would be excused, so the daughter could say what she disagreed with versus what she did not agree with.

The mother was forthright as usual. She said that her daughter barricaded herself in the bathroom. The mother called 911. The police broke down the door. The patient had superficial scratches on both arms. The patient agreed to be admitted. That was about it.

Now I was astonished. The daughter talked to me freely. She said that she had made three attempts to kill herself but God would not let her. She said it was time to stop being stupid. She was grateful she had a mother who was a very good nurse and a father elsewhere she telephoned every day. She said she had a good job at a restaurant. She said she wanted to go back to school and study to be an obstetrician, or at least a nurse.

I could not believe she could laugh and smile about how stupid she had been. She chose to continue her anti-depressant and to allow her mother to give her a lorazepam, but not more than once a day. She respected her therapist who would level with her. She respected me for the same reason. She knew she was a borderline and she would set up a blog to teach about being a borderline.

I could not believe what a good patient she was being compared to the one who would not talk with me at all for months. Could she really have reversed her downward course of despair? It seemed she had, but I also could not believe it. I had a double take.

That night I learned the next day she had called about losing her job, but not being suicidal, and willing to come in if she was suicidal. She just wanted to know how to get a lawyer to sue the restaurant. So she was only partly better. It was a start. Her judgment was clearly adolescent.

Hard lessons come hard. Addicts deal them out to us. Last in the day and late, such a patient "came to get my medications." She said she had not had them for a year, because she had no insurance. Now she had the insurance. I noticed in her chart that she had a history of cocaine abuse. I asked her about it. She blew it off as past history, not relevant. One of the three was a fairly high dose of a benzodiazepine, alprazolam to be precise. The other two were no problem, sertraline and quetiapine, neither a controlled substance.

I told her my nurse would take care of these three substances in the morning. Well, my double take at the end of the day did not sit well with me. My back felt uncomfortable. I did not want to think about it, the shadow side of this patient. My back was trying to tell me something, but I was not ready to listen.

At 4 AM I woke up and rethought the situation. No way was I going to prescribe a controlled substance to a patient with a history of cocaine addiction! Her blowing it off as irrelevant past history was actually quite relevant. My double take knew it, but it took over night for my 2nd impression to become completely clear.

I will try my best not to act immediately on 1st impressions. Some are fraught with a shadow that can get me in big trouble. It is tempting to move too fast. Our species is extremely vulnerable to jumping in too fast. That is Part IV of this book.

Once you have warned yourself are you out of danger? Hardly! Last evening I read to my wife from Henry Beston (1928) about the intensity of the summer on Cape Cod in his beautiful sentences. Then I chose the program played in 2008 of the Berlin Philharmonic of American music that was incredibly moving. In the right tempo each piece from George Gershwin, Samuel Barber, Aaron Copland, John Adams and Jerome Kern was right each in its own different way.

I was still hearing the music at 2 AM but I felt a warning flush chill of the opposite coming. When? I woke up in the coming nightmare at 6 AM. It was about being back at the beautiful farm of my roommate in Harvard College. I admired this Gun Mill Farm and I admired my roommate's father the doctor.

Admiring is dangerous. In the dream I was trying to find paper to write thanks to my roommate's parents before I left, but all the paper had already been written on. I found but one piece of paper I could write on, wrote on it and left and then noticed I had not left the message as I intended. I went back and left it and starting walking in a snow fog and had to wake up. I probably had felt a double take the moment I met this family.

References

Beston, H.: *The Outermost House, A Year On The Great Beach Of Cape Cod* (1928). New York: St. Martin's Griffin, 1988.

Freud, S.: The antithetical meaning of primal words. *The Standard Edition of the Complete Psychological Works of Sigmund Freud* (1910), Volume 11, pp. 153–161. London: Hogarth Press, 1953.

Gustafson, J.: *The New Interpretation of Dreams*. Madison, Wisconsin: James Gustafson Publisher, 1997.

Hughes, T.: *Winter Pollen*. London: Faber and Faber, 1997.

James, W.: *The Varieties of Religious Experience (Gifford Lectures 1901–1902)*. New York: The Modern Library, 1999.

Dreams And Myths As Second Impression

Chapter 7	The Pivot Of The Night Painting As Second Impression
Chapter 8	A Step From Walking Off A Cliff
Chapter 9	Imagining What Has Not Been Imagined

7

The Pivot Of The Night Painting As Second Impression

Your advantage in reading this chapter could be your waking up to the teacher inside you. Dreams are our best teachers. They can confirm or disconfirm 1st impressions held at bedtime.

For example, I had a patient whose wife was cold to him. He kept hoping she would be warm. He had a very useful dream in reply to this hope. He dreamed of turning on the hot water, but it stunk like phosphorus. This dream was hard, but true. Perhaps nothing else would prove it to him. Teachers need to be hard sometimes to save us from pouring out energy to lost causes.

For example, I had another patient who spent her life taking care of others. She dreamed of taking care of herself. Picturing it brought it home to her that she could change her life.

The geometry of crossings can be very difficult because you cannot see or read all of the forces. General Grant found this out when Lincoln appointed him General of the Union forces of the Potomac. He let loose his forces. The Confederates were ready for this and killed a huge number of his troops. Grant seemed to have learned to hold back from 1st impressions from here on in the war. He could wait for 2nd impressions before he moved.

Dreams, however, can be false. Penelope had waited for Odysseus to return from the war for ten years. Unknown to her, Odysseus had already returned disguised as a poor beggar in the eighteenth chapter of the *Odyssey*. She confided in this beggar that she had had a dream that Odysseus would return. However, she knew that dreams coming from the gates of ivory could be false wish fulfillments never to be granted. She also knew that dreams coming from the gates of horn could be true. She said to the beggar that she did not know which was the case. The beggar replied that he had heard that Odysseus was coming. This stirred her hopes.

Dreams can be performances of characters stepping back into being their heroic predecessors to summon their confidence (Mann, 1937). Quijote did this over and over again to summon the confidence of his predecessor knight of the Middle Ages (Cervantes, 1605).

Lévi-Strauss (Gustafson, chapter in *The New Interpretation of Dreams* called "The orchestral score of Lévi-Strauss," 1997) wrote that the tribes of South America depended on myths (shared dreams) that allowed them to make the dangerous transitions they were subject to, like leaving the wet season for the dry season or like enjoying the sweet fruits that would turn rotten. Their survival depended upon reading these transitions rightly. Failure to make these transitions could destroy them. In other words, the failure to make these transitions when their time had come would be tragic for the tribe.

Canetti elaborated a related strength of myth for Ice Age humanity beautifully in his book, *Crowds and Power* (1960). Male humanity ran in small packs that imitated wolves. Their action were as hunting packs, war packs, lamentation packs and increase backs.

Women had their own wolf imitation. I had a patient who loved coming to my office for all of the calendars that had wolf faces staring out into the distance. She felt herself to be a wolf. Like them she was shy. On the other hand she had good eyes for things far away she needed to reckon.

Freud (1900) wrote that day residues were worked into night dreams. I find this to be especially true when one or more of my patients disturb me. It allows me a 2nd impression in a dream, a night picture as it were, so I can understand what is getting into me and insisting on being recognized.

For example, I had several patients in one day in the clinic that longed for company in their pain. My night picture told me they were not going to get it. I pictured a group of guys wading a trout stream together with an old wooden bridge over the stream that gave way and I started to fall through it. In other words, the longing would not hold up in reality. The night picture is this kind of thinking in pictures.

For another example, I had several patients in one day in the clinics that were being bullied into submission by their spouses. Some gave in. Some fought back. I had a picture of a gun being put to my head. In other words, many marriages start with violence from the first date that only gets worse and worse over time. My night picture of thinking says to watch out for the first step. Many people have little experience with symmetry and equality in a relationship. It gets harder and harder over time to start over.

Jesus was talking to his disciples about their privilege of knowing the kingdom of heaven versus those not knowing about the kingdom of heaven. I am talking about symmetry and equality in a relationship or marriage as a kind of kingdom of heaven known by the fortunate. To them shall be given.

Is the dream necessary for presenting a 2nd impression? No, it is only necessary for time to pass for daytime or nighttime contemplation to have their say. Jim Donovan (personal communication) posed a series of questions to me about this that I found very clarifying as follows.

First, how is one to learn to heed the dream message? I suggest writing down a few sentences at bedtime that will line up the conscious with the unconscious. On starting to awaken, I suggest just to make mental notes before opening one's eyes or moving one's head. Then sitting up, write the notes down. They need not be dreams, but they usually come from deep down and are uncanny in their relevance.

Second, about a hundred and twenty years after Freud, what can be added to his method? Freud's basic technique was to follow the free associations to the dream elements into the unconscious. What goes farther, I find, is to take the dream as an analogy or metaphor. As Alfred Margulies wrote in *The Empathic Imagination* (1989), the dream analogy or metaphor puts you into the position of the patient for discussion with him or her.

Third, is it possible that patients will test you unconsciously whether you have dangerous characteristics of the parent or not? Yes.

Recently, I have written a very brief essay for *Psychodynamic Practice* (Gustafson, 2019) that will illustrate all of these points. I was consulting to a resident or junior doctor and her beautiful patient who kept leaving her bullying husband and their two children, only to come back after a short time.

My 1st impression was like that of the resident. Guilt drove her patient back. The more I sat with the two of them, the more I had a 2nd impression. The mother was a very good mother, but her husband talked to her so badly in front of the children that she lost all confidence. I was on the right track.

As I was waking up the day after the consultation, I found myself on a chessboard in brilliant light where there was no place for cover. The mother's situation penetrated me. I wrote the mother a note describing my nightmare on her behalf. This allowed her to see just how terrible it was to continue in the husband's harsh game.

Unconsciously she was testing whether I would be dangerously like her parents to minimize the nightmare of the marriage. I named it for what it was in my nightmare. Then she could name it objectively for herself. She left her husband finally forever and got custody of the children. She had done almost all of the work and she had done it well. She had been talked out of it. Now she was not going to allow that to happen again.

This is the pivotal action of 2nd impressions. I had been looking at the situation of the patient as caused by her guilt. This was partly true. Now I saw it also as the crushing of her confidence by the husband on his chessboard, so to speak, in brilliant light with no place for cover. My nightmare supplied this pivoting to a radically different idea. The mother and I were in this together. Accurate analogies and metaphors bring about radical empathy.

I had a dream about this. I dreamed that I was quite young as at the beginning of my career as a professor, only the time was now. I would have to get grants to support my salary and I would have to interview large numbers of subjects for my research and I would have to employ very complicated statistics for my conclusions. This did not sound good in the dream itself.

I gladly woke up to get out of it! I thought to myself that I have all the subjects I need in my caseload. Some of the patients do not have access to their dreams and some do have access to their dreams in 2nd impressions.

For example, I had a man who was always told he was wrong as a child. It did not stop. His mother continued it. He had no money to get away from this mother. I could barely stand listening to it. He got something out of our meeting. He could feel anger and even hatred. That was a pivot. His anger and hatred was justified. No matter he could not tell his mother this. This would only provoke shouting between them. I sensed he felt more real and accepted as such.

For another example, I had a woman who always was wrong as a child. This is why she never stopped telling me how great she was. She felt compelled. I saw her as little as possible. I doubt if she understood that most people tried to see her as little as possible. At least, when I saw her again, I would know what to expect, the same show.

I find dreamers more imaginative and interesting in their surprising 2nd impressions. One did not think she ever dreamed. I persisted in saying to her that she must have dreamed once. She shook her head over and over again. Finally, near the conclusion of our one-hour consultation, she said she had had a senseless dream. It was that there was a murderer in the family.

The Pivot Of The Night Painting

She was certain this was completely senseless. I doubted it. She had made a curious remark when we were setting up the video equipment making a video for teaching the residents. I had commented that our video room was more like a movie studio. She retorted, "Then where is the Lion?" She meant the MGM (Metro Golden Mayer) movie business whose movies always began with a picture of this lion turning his head back and forth.

To make a long story short, it turned out she was going marry a man whose father was in the Lion's Club. The father pretended to be honorable, but he was full of deceit and sleeping with other women who were not his wife. In other words, he was a false Lion. She was glad that she and her fiancé could discuss him and see him as little as possible. She could even discuss her anger that this father was trying to get full custody of her fiancé's younger brother when the mother was indeed the good mother. As we completed her hour of consultation, she remarked that murderers do not belong in families. This simple sentence was a pivotal second impression for her.

If that dream was as difficult as possible to get, the dream of another patient was quite ready to spring out as a great pivot. I saw her for an hour's consultation with a resident about whether to get married or not to her fiancé. She had told her fiancé to move out prior to the consultation and delayed the wedding.

She was quite disgusted with her fiancé but she was equivocating about whether to be finished with him or not. I sensed that she, nearly thirty years old, feared she would never have another proposal for marriage. I sensed her parents feared she would end up an old maid. The fiancé was, thus, their choice. Her father even coached the fiancé how to boss her like he did.

The dream was startling, a pivotal action. She dreamed she was walking in the corridors of a hospital. She came to the top of a staircase that looked down to the door of a delivery room. Suddenly, the doors swung open and her mother and father and fiancé came through it. She exclaimed: "My mother has given birth to my fiancé!" She laughed. She was definitely not going to spend her life taking care of her mother's infant.

At this point in composing my book, I waited for my own dream that would indicate what needed to be developed next. At midnight that very night, my sieve replied with a dream. I dreamed that Sándor Ferenzi, one of Freud's close followers, came to give a lecture on the great use of dreams. He gave me a Xerox copy. However, only the psychoanalysts could sit on the left side of the audience. Those of us who are not psychoanalysts could only sit of the right side of the audience.

49

I knew at once that a second dream would follow later in the night. It came as a nightmare. I dreamed I was a batter in softball, but there was no place to bat from. There was only a big hole where one would expect a home plate and batter's boxes. Was I very disturbed? Yes, I was. Did I think of refraining from trying to bat? Yes, I did think of that.

No place to bat from? Yet expected to bat? That sounds like a set up for catastrophe. But what disaster? I thought of several possibilities. One is the disaster of patients who cannot face the 2nd impression of having no place to stand. Rather such patients run around attempting to be busy in their outer world, so they do not even pause to contemplate their own feelings let alone their dreams that are nightmares.

Why was Ferenczi giving this lecture on the great use of dreams, with psychoanalysts on the left side of the auditorium and non-psychoanalysts on the right side of the auditorium? And why did he give me a Xerox of his lecture? And no one else! I am not a psychoanalyst.

I think he was calling on me at midnight to carry on a great tradition of the use of dreams. I was chosen. That changed my book. I saw that I needed to bring forth the most important knowledge to cope with dreams. I had left out this education for my readers.

For example, most of my readers had not read Erik Erikson's brilliant essay called "The dream specimen of psychoanalysis" (1954). For example, most of my readers had not read Alfred Margulies' book, *The Empathic Imagination* (1989) and his subsequent development. It is high time to make a short list of the invaluable contributions and explicate what we can borrow from them.

As for Erikson's thoughts on this subject, he saw many dimensions for looking at dream specimens. I count thirty or more as follows: taken singly, time, space, movement, the interpersonal crowd, affects, words, history, conflict-free regions, color, shading, trigger, transference, holes and social status, and taking combined, synesthesia, spatial zoom, the crowd of characters, the actions of the dreamer, the religious dimensions, the group psychology, awakening and sleeping in the dream, stages of life, reverberation of old weak points, nakedness and clothing, the central point or navel, the muse of the dream, the pulling apart of the self, the dream played backwards, the range between the point of fixation and the point of arrest, evil and moral mission (Gustafson, 1997, pp. 82 and 83, 1997). One was the S [E] I N E dream in which the dreamer was reducing her dream to none of the dimensions Erikson knew about. She was reducing herself to nothing. That was her style.

I had such a dream myself. I had it the night after I glimpsed Kamala Harris destroy Joe Biden in the first Democratic Party debate. I had a double take on how beautifully she did it and yet I feared for her life. She reminded me of Martin Luther King. King was a charismatic authority that moved crowds and yet King got shot on a balcony and killed.

I had a disturbed night. I dreamed I was giving a very terse and tough message at a press concert. I made myself inconspicuous. That was the style of this dream, not quite as radical as the S [E] I N E dreamer who made herself nothing. Inconspicuous is a style of modesty unlikely to attract any attention, good or bad. Style may be the most important aspect of a speech or of a dream. I adopted it out of fear for myself.

Another that leaps to mind is the essay by Franz Alexander (1925) on pairs of dreams and how they work as double takes. Another is what Carl Jung brought to us that are quite different from what Freud brought.

I can see I have some work to do. I am just beginning to contemplate what I need to reread so my readers can borrow what is the very best.

What about Jung's contributions to reading dreams? Are they not many, and is this many not of one piece? Have I not spent decades on this problem and fourteen books, counting this one? For me, Jung's contributions to reading dreams comes down to a pair of sentences from Wallace Stevens (1997) as follows: "It is a violence from within that protects us from a violence from without. It is the imagination pressing back against the pressure of reality (p. 665)."

I noticed my many 1st impressions as follows: Jung was good at estimations of others being too low or too high. The latter got the reduction to absurdity. Jung was good at recognizing the appearances of the gods and the sacred in dreams. Was this not unprecedented? It was precedented in the Old Testament. Recall the dream of Joseph on the seven fat cattle followed by the seven thin fallow cattle coming out of the water. From this Joseph could warn the Pharaoh what he was to expect in the next seven years of plenty and store up wheat for what followed in the seven years of famine.

Jung was also good at mandalas he started drawing in 1918 while he was an officer in the reserve army on drills. He found the mandalas would lose their balance, exaggerating the horizontal or the vertical, until they got their balance back. Jung was also good at helping Wolfgang Pauli, the physicist who won the Nobel Prize for the Pauli exclusion principle. Pauli had many hundreds of dreams. Jung had a young colleague see Pauli while Jung carefully examined Pauli's dreams. He argued that Pauli was engaged in what Jung called "circumlocution of the center." This, Jung argued, was a way to correct the distortions of his mandalas, first one, then another, and so forth.

Finally, on my 1st impression of Jung, I found he was quite alert to archetypes that take over most people. This was not a good thing.

On rereading my study of Jung in my books, I found a number of 2nd impressions that led me to seeing how all of Jung was quite consistent. He was aware of the shadow, always available to compensate the persona with what was missing in the picture. Jung was also good at seeing dilemmas, like the daughter who could save herself but not her mother in hell. It was one or the other.

Jung was also good at seeing what he called "regressive restoration of the persona" to flee the archaic vitality that primordial image that would otherwise take over. Jung was also good at summarizing the whole situation: Running from the primitive back to the absolute banal of the persona or becoming the mouthpiece of the primitive.

Finally, Jung was very good at recognizing the modern machine and staying clear of it in his retreat at Bolligen at the Upper Lake Zurich, learning from his suffering being too close to World War I and ready not to suffer it so closely in World War II. In between he had a beautiful dream of being in Liverpool with six other Swiss in the fog and dirt and dross. They climbed into its heights to discover a beautiful circle in which a red magnolia shone in the sun or itself emitted its glorious light. Thus he discovered it was possible to have an imagination pressing back against the pressure of reality, as Wallace Stevens would say.

Would you like something charming? Listen to this! Franz Alexander (1925 and Gustafson 1997) has something for you. He had a dream in two parts. The first part is about the patient and his brother being pelted with stones by the boatman, from whom they flee. The second part is about a little girl asking the patient to kiss her in a difficult place to reach in her elbow. He and his brother used to kiss their mother in exactly this place.

Is it not pure Freud? 1st impression, the repression! 2nd impression, the lovely gratification of kissing the little girl/mother in the secret and difficult place of the elbow! It is precisely what Freud thought the dream instrument was about.

I have since seen that opposite pairs of dreams like this are commonplace. If I have a harsh dream earlier in the night, I am very likely to have a lovely dream later. If I have a lovely dream early, I am very likely to have a harsh dream later. Our unconscious seems to want to ready us for either extreme.

Now Alfred Margulies (1989) was up to something far more complex that I will do my best to explain to you. Margulies and I had Elvin Semrad for our first teacher. Semrad was a genius of empathy that could reach just about any patient residents or we medical students could bring to him. Margulies also had a great literary education as I did, allowing him to center on Proust in his capacity to focus on a sensory detail and Gerard Manley Hopkins in his beautiful concept of the inscape peculiar to each individual.

Now, thirty years after I first read *The Empathic Imagination* (1989), I have studied his book again. It is not about dream work per se. I do think it changes dream work in a salutary way.

For me, his concluding *Epilogue Beyond Metaphor* makes a beautiful and profound summary of his book. He tells of coming back from being away to being back with his four year old daughter to tell stories at bedtime. She asks her father for a story on bunny rabbits.

"The daddy bunny," I said, "was going away for a few days, but he'd soon be back."

"Why was he going?" Oh, to look around, see some different carrot patches. Bunnies like carrots you know." She thought about this, it seemed plausible. "Oh, I bet I know what he brought back." Carrots I thought – but her answer was better: "He brought home a carrot T-shirt." We had exchanged T-shirts, one real, one metaphoric, both ways of connecting to one another (1989, p. 145).

This reminds me of our dream group coming back every two weeks to connect with one another. The first presenter of three presenters per session tells us her or his dream, thinks about it out loud with us and receives our 2nd impressions to discuss back and forth. She or he discovers herself and we discover her or him, like Alfred and his daughter. Our empathy for one another becomes deeper and wider through exploration with each presenter of her or his inscape.

Extending inscapes is not necessarily a good idea. This can be too painful in its truth. Semrad could always find and bear intolerable pain with our patients when we brought them in and his presence is what made it possible. Our invitations to our entire department to join us do not enlarge our group beyond about five of us. Why? Being known at a deep level seems to be too vulnerable for most people. It is far safer to fit into convention to belong like everyone else.

My wife is a violinist and an author on how different kinds of music flow into each other. We take turns choosing to watch and listen to the Berlin Philharmonic every evening and we have our own dream group of the two of us every morning. She asked me a very interesting question, "Are there musical dreams?" I replied on 1st impression that I never heard of one. On 2nd impression, I thought surely she must be right that great composers hear their original compositions waking up. That very evening I chose *Pictures at an Exhibition* composed by Mussorgsky and orchestrated by Ravel, one of our favorites. It moved me such that it sang in me all night. I dreamed she and I were completing the details in the construction of a beautiful hall in rhythm with *Pictures at an Exhibition*. Musical dreams are possible!

References

Alexander, F.: Dreams in pairs and series. *International Journal of Psychoanalysis* 1925; 446–450.

Canetti, E.: *Crowds and Power* (1960). New York: Farrar, Straus and Giroux, 1984.

Erikson, E.: The dream specimen of psychoanalysis. *Journal of the American Psychoanalytic Association* 1954; 2, 5–54.

Freud, S.: *Collected Works*, Volume IV. London: Hogarth Press, 1990.

Gustafson, J.: The orchestral score of Lévi-Strauss in *The New Interpretation of Dreams*. Madison, Wisconsin: James Gustafson Publisher, 1997.

Gustafson, J.: Second impressions. *Psychodynamic Practice*, Volume 25, June 2019.

Mann, T.: *Freud, Goethe and Wagner*. New York: Alfred A. Knopf, 1937.

Margulies, A.: *The Empathic Imagination*. New York: W.W. Norton, 1989.

Stevens, W.: *The Noble Rider in his Collected Poetry and Prose*. New York: The Library of America, 1997.

8

A Step From Walking Off A Cliff

Your advantage in reading this chapter could supply you with warnings and even dire warnings when you need them about what you are doing or where you are going.

Cormac McCarthy (2017) wrote that the unconscious cares about two things. One was to warn of catastrophes one step away. The second was to picture creations that had never been imagined before. He called it *The Kekulé Problem*. The latter occurred to Kekulé in his dream of a snake swallowing its own tail. He had been struggling a long time about the structure of benzene. The dream pictured the benzene ring he could never have imagined consciously.

McCarthy wrote that the other thing the unconscious cares about is to give advance warning of emergencies.

I had a patient who received such an advance warning in a dream, of being a step from walking off a chair with a noose around her neck. The scene was imagined to take place in the warehouse of the company my patient worked for. She was standing on this chair with a noose around her neck, surrounded by bosses and fellow workers that had been mean to her. Strangely to her, she found it was difficult to lift off the noose from her neck. It felt something like a comfortable blanket she had grown used to. It was her security blanket that made her a lot of money. She had followed the advice of her mother to stay with making a lot of money. On the other hand, to step off the chair with the noose on her neck was to destroy her identity. Her situation was exactly like that of the five patients described by Breuer and Freud in *Studies On Hysteria* (1990). Breuer and Freud wrote that all five patients were suffering from self-strangulation of their voices of objection.

She woke up with this dilemma (Gustafson, 2014) and was absolutely clear she would not allow herself to step into self-strangulation. She loved her voice. Indeed her dream a few weeks later took place in the same warehouse with the tables turned. She was walking up and down flashing a pair of scissors in front of the same bosses and co-workers who had been cruel to her. She was pronouncing the fates of each one of them. One was to be crucified on a cross, another to be drowned, a third to get a lethal injection and the fourth to be burned to death on a funeral pyre.

Of course, I did not want to bring forth such revenge! I helped her use her sharp, scintillating force to get out of this business and seek another that would make better use of her remarkable talents.

Another patient had a similar dramatic dream. His was of sighting a long line of barracudas facing out to the vast ocean of the Internet. He had fallen for several hours into a deal from the Internet that would be very harmful to him. Once again, the picture of what was going on woke up the patient.

I had another patient who had a similar dramatic dream warning, two nights in a row. The first night was about being hit by a golf ball on a famous course. Then this guy sighted him as not belonging there, a colonel like the one in Faulkner's (1939) short story, "Barn Burning," and told never again to be seen there. It made him feel like a low life.

The next night there was a similar guy in his dream who was operating a big machine, kind of like a road grader. He sat up high on a big seat in the back and directed it wherever he wanted. However, the great machine was very vulnerable to getting tangled up in wool thread. When it did happen, he could pay off the workers with a small bribe like thirty-five cents, again making the workers feel like low life.

The next time he operated it, someone dropped a whole wool sweater in his path that stopped his machine altogether. He was in a rage, again like the colonel in "Barn Burning." Such righteous bullies are everywhere in American life like our so-called president, ready to dismiss losers. Winners like him brook no opposition. My patient was put on alert for the next Guy.

A third night in a row continued this sequence of dreams about fire and ice. It reminded me of Robert Frost's (1920) poem, "Fire and Ice." Frost saw ahead to what was coming. My patient saw ahead also. Jung found that sequences of dreams were very telling.

This third night gave him a pair of dreams: The first of the pair was about fire coming. My patient knew it was time to leave the land. It reminded him of the tragedy of Paradise (California) on fire. Many did not get out in time.

The second of the pair was about a baseball game. Men were on first and second base with no out. Bunting was not a good idea. The opponents were already close in for a bunt. The coach was on fire and went to the plate himself, exclaiming: "Johnny Slaughter is going to hit this one hard." The rival coach objected that coaches do not bat for their teams. The first coach agreed. He said his cool black guy was going to bat instead of himself.

My patient was reminded of singing in Brahms' *German Requiem* (1868). He recalled the conductor's introduction of himself in rehearsal. We must have hearts on fire, heads like ice.

Everyone that has sung in choirs or played sports knows that fiery conductors or coaches make a mess of things. They lack a balance between having fire and staying cool. This is a vital position for fresh play and even originality or creation.

The dream instrument practices balance in pairs of dreams. One nightmare can be followed by one beautiful dream or vice versa. One nightmare of predators can be followed by one dream of foraging and vice versa. This is the Lotka Scenario. Be ready for what you want but also for what you do not want. Many biologists call this the engine of evolution. It selects fit animals. Unfortunately the end of the Ice Age began the selection of specialists, as of one crop like rice (Harari, 2014). Nowadays this is mostly how you get paid for filing income tax or prescribing drugs. Fit for anything else?

Sunday to Monday dreams, looking towards work as a doctor, ought not to be taken literally. It seems that having a fine weekend makes the unconscious bring up the opposite that things could be dire.

I had this typical one. I was a counselor at a boys' camp totally out of control. What kind of adults would they become? I wanted nothing to do with it at 3 AM.

At 6 AM, I dreamed I was back in Saginaw, Michigan where I was born and grew up until I went to Cambridge to MIT for one year and then Harvard College for three years and then four years at Harvard Medical School. In my dream I was wading through two feet of snow until I reached West Michigan Avenue that was full of low businesses and rich people. I finally found a guy who pointed where I could catch a bus to go back where I came from. Strangely, Lake Michigan was to my right and a sign for Gerald Ford was to my left. He was from Grand Rapids.

In other words, my pair of dreams was disoriented in so many ways. My practice with the residents and their patients the next day was merely banal and not difficult at all. I actually was quite well oriented. I was not one step from walking off a cliff.

I suppose I could have been in danger from being disoriented. I was not in danger as it turned out. The unconscious can foresee things coming as in Shakespeare's *Richard the Second* warnings of being murdered before dawn. It is not always veridical. The unconscious seems to bring up possibilities like my pair of dreams, especially after I have had a very good weekend. It can simply be worrying about the whole week as a doctor. I am in it and cannot know in advance what could be extremely difficult like being one step from walking off a cliff.

It seems like my unconscious wants me not to ride too high into the week. It works for a kind of humility that is not too cocky. That is its effect. When you have gone away to MIT and Harvard College and then Harvard Medical School, you have seen hosts of the so-called best and the so-called brightest.

You try your best not to act like them. As Rumsfeld said, the greatest problems of national security are not the knowns or the known unknowns, but rather the unknown unknowns. After all, I had no forewarning that Notre Dame de Paris would erupt in flames two weeks ago. It was unthinkable and it happened.

We have had a dream group in our Department of Psychiatry for several years organized by Stuart Jones and myself. Being in it every two weeks is a profound privilege. In every meeting, we find time for the presentation and discussion of three dreams of three dreamers. I can say it is always profound because all the dreams signal serious warnings. From these, we are taught.

Now I do not intend to betray the confidentiality of my peers. I can tell you something very interesting about our being a step from walking off a cliff. Our dreams are like ancient myths. They are all about pivoting away from peril by sighting where things are going and thus being able save oneself in a radically different direction. They are like the myths of Greek tragedy and they are like the myths of South American Indian tribes.

In classical Greece these disasters were enacted in the Greek outdoor theatres. Usually the cause was what they called hubris, excessive confidence. Oedipus is the most well known. His father Laius, the king of Thebes, drove Oedipus off the road when Laius was passing through on his chariot. Oedipus killed him in rage. This event set in motion a plague. Oedipus now the King sought the murderer of Laius, being unwitting that the murderer had been himself.

I do not pretend that our nightmares presented are of this magnitude. Rather they are more like the myths of the South American Indian tribes (Lévi-Strauss, 1969). For those tribes, the dangers, not to be overlooked, were concerned with the radical changes the tribes had to undergo, like wet to dry, raw to cooked, fresh to rotten, abundant to scarce, and so forth.

I gave an example in the previous chapter of my dream at midnight of my being chosen to carry on the knowledge of the great uses of the dream. Towards dawn my excessive confidence was brought up short. I had a nightmare of trying to be a batter in softball, but there was no home plate and no batter's boxes, only a big hole! I had no place to stand. I was not going to be able hit anything if that was my situation.

You could say I had some excessive confidence, or Greek hubris. You could say that I was like the South American Indian in having to anticipate that sometimes I was privileged to teach the great uses of dreams, but sometimes I had no such audience or I had many patients unable to face their own nightmares.

Modern conditions are somewhat different. For us the common trouble is having way too much information and way too much material. It happened to me, for sure. I had the habit of tacking up things of interest to me to the white walls of my study and staircase. It took thirty or forty years for me to catch on that I was just getting in my own way. I had a devil of a time taking all of this material down, leaving a very few pictures, mostly of our family.

Harry Stack Sullivan (1956) and D. W. Winnicott (1971) were very keen at letting patients know what material was useless. Sullivan would show his disinterest by making transitions, smooth when the patient could listen, accented when the patient needed Sullivan to be somewhat sharp in his emphasis and abrupt when the patient was going to run on endlessly.

Winnicott was more tolerant with children in his squiggle game of drawing lines and having the child complete the drawing and give it a name. Then the child would go first and Winnicott complete it and give it a name. For some while the child would draw very conventional objects like houses, cars and so forth. Often the fun of it allowed the child to become more daring. As Winnicott would say, now things were hanging fire, and so he would say to the child that he probably had had a dream about all this and often they did.

Winnicott did not offer such sessions until the parents had much confidence in him. Then the child would borrow that confidence and would start to have dreams of this being the right doctor for him or her. That would be the sacred moment to offer a session. Often the child's dream would go right back to his or her being hurt. Often it was when the mother was having another child and the child patient felt abandoned.

To pull together a number of strands, children can have felt like they were a step from walking off cliffs, or left on them, and there is much material that would get nowhere near this, as they hide in conventionality that is all surface cover up. With the confidence of the parents, borrowed by the child, Winnicott knew how to move deep gradually in the company of the child in one-hour consultations.

To be sure, adults can also be left on cliffs while hiding in conventionality rushing around with agendas that are too much, with too much information and with too much material. Sullivan taught us how to change the subject with his smooth, accented and abrupt transitions.

Have you ever heard of couples, like husband and wife, being striking warning systems? They can be exceptionally profound in their alertness like dream groups. I will give you a nightmare example from one of my patients and from his report of his wife's parallel nightmare.

According to my patient, his nightmare began with his staying an hour late at his business to participate in the togetherness exercises of his new young staff. To his surprise, his wife showed up looking abandoned and desolate. He promised to come home in ten minutes while he skated with his young people.

When he got home, again shocked, he found his wife driving a jeep that had no top. At first he was driving his own car that could not be stopped. Somehow he managed to stop it.

In the morning, shocked again, he listened to his wife tell of her nightmare of being at a kind of county fair of crazy rides. She got belted in one of those speeded up rides. Going faster and faster, noticing that no one was controlling the ride, she had to wake up and take in no more of this craziness.

In listening to this pair of nightmares of husband and wife, each about the desperate situation of the wife, I was struck by how the pair of nightmares was alarming in different ways. Did they not agree? I thought they did. The husband and wife were able to discuss these two analogies. They agreed the wife had to do something different. She did not have to stay belted to a ride going faster and faster without anyone going to stop it or driving a jeep with no top and he driving his own car with no brakes.

My wife and I tried out this alarm system for us. I had a nightmare about the most evil man in the world. I tricked him and then I stabbed him in his larynx. Well, evil, how do you tempt anyone after that? That was my 1st impression, that I could put evil out of business!

Alas, I had a double take. Immediately, I sensed that his toxic evil could not be buried for long as at Love Canal. It would come up and destroy much of the town!

My wife had a similar dream about a psychotic boy we know. She dreamed that she could keep him controlled in a restaurant. It sat uneasily in her. She knew better.

Could I face the ancient problem of Kekulé myself? I began to contemplate Kekulé's dream once again. The structure of benzene was his aim. It seemed to be unknown to everyone. His dream was about a serpent swallowing its tail. Is that not about as evil as you can get? The ring hiding the evil?

In the Garden of Eden, was it not the serpent that tempted Eve to tempt Adam with the knowledge of good and evil? Did he not fall for it? Beautiful and tough and astute women have been known to do this many times since Eve!

So here is my 2nd impression. As Jung demonstrated over and over again, a smooth and pretty face can hide its shadow for a long time. Beware!

Is it not one step from walking off a cliff? Her husband will kill you. Or you will kill yourself. Freud called it the Oedipus Complex.

You see, if you can bear seeing it, that the shadow of evil can be denied. Try denying it as long as you can!

My second You Tube lecture (about ten minutes long) was about what Freud said about dreams and what Jung said about dreams and what I say about dreams. I dreamed of being on a Greek island with my wife. It seemed secure. The heat came on so fast in the mornings that we had to dive into the ocean for relief. It was like Troy that also seemed to be secure to the Trojans. It seemed like the room in which I gave this lecture was also secure. A killer could come through the door to the room anytime. A voice droned, "They are coming, sooner or later."

Could psychiatry have no interest in the forces of evil? It seems not. What? Did they never hear about the collapse of identity and the resultant struggle between God and the Devil for the capture of the soul? William James lectured about it in 1901 and 1902 in Edinburgh. Who in psychiatry has ever heard of William James and his famous book? I have heard about it and I wrote about it in my thesis at Harvard Medical School with respect to auditory hallucinations in chronic paranoid schizophrenia. I had my set of patients in Edinburgh and Boston take down diaries of what their voices said. Each was entirely a struggle between God and the Devil. I described in my book, *The Common Dynamics of Psychiatry* (Gustafson, 1999).

Could evil no longer be a force that we have to reckon with? Do we only need to administer anti-psychotics and pay attention to the QT prolongation on the EKG? I am not against the latter. I have to do it. Can we not also talk with such patients about their struggle with evil?

Mind you, neurotics also have to struggle mightily with evil. Dread of contamination is the most obvious example of fear of evil taking over. Mind you, I do not consider myself much of a neurotic, but I did have that nightmare I told you about already of my tricking and stabbing the most evil man ever in his larynx so he could tempt no more souls. Then I feared his toxic juices coming back up as happened at Love Canal to do terrible damage.

Evil can be denied as a force but it is irrepressible. My book you are reading could be rightly said to be about nothing else. Our neighborhood is having a terrible time struggling with evil. What goes on in families or between husband and wife tends to be just awful. The politics of our country is so beset by evil, or one might say Trumpistan, that no one knows if it will be saved or not.

Come to think more about this, evil and terrible forces are but one concern of what Gedo called the hierarchy of aims (Gedo, 1979, Gustafson, 1986, Chapter 9). The unconscious will oscillate between concern for one aim and the other important aims.

At 2 AM last night, I had a nightmare about a UW Building. The tall part was visibly engulfed in flame and the lower part not yet. I was able to go into the lower building and urge about ten students to get out at once, but three would not heed me so I gave up on them and fled. Just then the tall part collapsed upon the lower part. This reminded me of the fires in Paradise this last summer and in Los Angeles and Napa Valley the previous summer, all in California. In these places, the moment to flee had to be seized or one would be dead.

Strikingly, my unconscious was giving me a most dire picture of alarming situations I must heed as a matter of life and death. Surprisingly, I fell asleep, sufficiently apprised of this kind of emergency.

Four hours later I had a dream picture about something quite beautiful I would want to engage with. There are many such things.

Four hours after that, my stomach was still distressed. Taking care of my body is another vital aim for me in my hierarchy. So I just let an hour pass for it to settle.

So this is how my unconscious will take care of me. It will oscillate like this among my chief aims. There is no other way my chief aims could be taken care of.

How could my unconscious be helping me by giving me a dreadful nightmare in the transition from Sunday to Monday going back to the department? Judge for yourself. I dreamed I was returning to a department of psychiatry in a big city. The chairman took me aside to tell me that a committee of three had reduced my salary because I was not seeing enough patients. He would do what he could, knowing as he did that I did a lot of psychotherapy that took more time and so I saw fewer patients. Would he? I was already late to start seeing patients and I was in a part of the department I had never seen before and I set off fire alarms several times unwittingly. Was I in trouble all ready? Yes, and it got worse. There were eight patients of eight residents waiting to see their cases. The first was a wildly seductive young woman who kept trying to put herself in my lap that I had to keep thrusting away from me. How was I to keep up with the other seven patients who were wildly violent, each worse than the previous one? Could I wake up?

Strangely, I did wake up and felt better that such a department was not mine. I felt grateful for the one I have got already. The unconscious has this way of helping by oscillating from terrible to actual. Gratitude for the actual reality you have got is a good attitude to start the week with.

Strangely, this was followed by a great dream. I was climbing a mountain, hands reaching up to the next grip and pulling myself up. Then I moved along a ledge sighting the upper mountain above me. Then I reached a small lodge where I was served a great trout supper. Watch out for grizzlies grabbing my trout! Go down the mountain before it gets dark! This reminds me of hiking in Italy forty years ago with some different details.

References

Freud, S.: *Collected Works*, Volume IV. London: Hogarth Press, 1990.

Gedo, J.: *Beyond Interpretation, Toward a Revised Theory for Psychoanalysis*. New York: International Universities Press, 1979.

Gustafson, J.: *The Complex Secret of Brief Psychotherapy*. New York: W.W. Norton, 1986.

Gustafson, J.: *The Common Dynamics of Psychiatry*. Madison. Wisconsin: James Gustafson Publisher, 1999.

Gustafson, J.: Collisions of the social body and the individual body in an hour's one-time consultation in Hoyt, M and Talmon, M: *Capturing the Moment*. Bethel, Connecticut: Crown Publishing, 2014.

Harari, Y.: *Sapiens, A Brief History of Humankind*. New York, Harper Collins, 2014.

James, W.: *The Varieties of Religious Experience*. New York: Modern Library, 1999.

Lévi-Strauss, C.: *The Raw and the Cooked.* Chicago: University of Chicago Press, 1969.

McCarthy, C.: The Kekulé problem. *Nautilus* (online), April 23, 2017.

Sullivan, H.S.: *Clinical Studies in Psychiatry.* New York: Norton, 1971.

Winnicott, D.W.: *Therapeutic Consultations in Child Psychiatry.* New York: Basic Books, 1971.

9

Imagining What Has Not Been Imagined

Your advantage in reading this chapter could be the power of creation, of things you never thought of.

In Chapter 8, we discussed how Kekulé performed this creation about the structure of benzene. Now we will consider another great contribution from Henri Poincaré in his essay "Mathematical creation" (1910) on this subject of creation.

It is the idea Poincaré had of his sieve. He was the father of non-linear geometry. It was not easy to compose his proofs. He could write out what a proof had to do, but there were millions of possibilities of where to start. What he did was to wait. He would hike on the ocean shore or in the forest and go about his other business when suddenly his sieve said: Start here!

He did not have the proof in hand. He had the place to start from that was promising. Indeed it was so, and one proof after another followed.

We all have a sieve. If we only knew of it! One of my patients was asked by her sister to sub taking care of their parents in Chicago. She did not want to do it. Her sieve came to her rescue. She could decline taking care of the parents. On the other hand, she would feel guilty declining. The guilt would gradually subside. This is creation, of something she had not done before.

I will give you an example of how my sieve worked to give me a 2nd impression after a very difficult day. I had one patient who was alarmed by himself. His wife told him she was going to divorce him because he was pushing her up against walls and saying degrading things to her. He had no memory of having done this. He called it a blackout.

He thought he had enacted what had been done to him as a young child about the age of their daughter. He said was taking his medication religiously to keep his manic tendencies under control. I told him this sounded more like dissociation. That is why he had no memory of having done it, like Dr. Jekyll had no memory of how Mr. Hyde marched around running over anyone in his path (Stevenson, 1888). He was terrified he might do this to his daughter. Could I give him another drug to prevent it? I said I did not know of such a drug, but that I would look into it.

The second patient in her twenties came in with her mother who was alarmed that her daughter might end up in a coma again by taking another huge overdose. She was discharged from inpatient psychiatry with little help. The daughter would not agree to any help at all. I felt helpless about this situation as much as the other one.

My sieve gave me a 2nd impression of my helplessness with a pair of nightmares. The first was that I was in a wooden city on fire, perhaps in a movie. I had to get out of there before the fire exploded (a non-linear jump).

The second nightmare was that I was choosing three bottles of red wine in a small French village in a very leisurely way. My father and a dead serious old colleague came along in a dump truck with a shovel in front of it. I was to get in the shovel and be tossed over the cab of the truck into its rear, like a garbage truck would do. I had to wake up.

The pair of dreams (Alexander, 1925) is all about time being rushed, interacting with Part IV of this book about the accelerating species we are. The detail of the dump truck interacts with Part I of this book of the detail showing the whole situation (Erikson's 1954 dream specimen). The choosing refers to the epigraph of my Preface: *To invent is to choose* (Poincaré 1910).

The harshness refers to that of these patients to themselves. I was picturing the harshness, as if I were each of the two patients. That is what Freud (1900) called a day residue. The left over flush and chill was what has been called a night residue (Leveton, 1961).

The creation of imagining what has not been imagined can also open up potential rather than clarify harshness. I had a patient who spent a very long time trying to get free of her family of origin and particularly free from her mother. Most of her energy had taken the form of anger at the family for putting her down. Her anger allowed her to go her own way. She stayed thousands of miles away from them. She was in fight/flight for most of her life.

Finally, when her mother was dying, she felt she was ready to visit her mother and her brothers and sisters. She felt the family could do whatever they wanted. She needed nothing from them.

Her mother did what she had always had done. Her mother said: "Don't ask me any questions!" My patient just laughed.

Having come back home here, she had a very beautiful dream. She dreamed that she was in a University of Art that opened up one beautiful kind of art after another. It was the biggest and most beautiful space she had ever been in. Now for the first time in her life she knew where her energies were going. As she said to me, her unconscious was much bigger than her conscious. In this great space, she would devote herself to being in her art of fabrics. It was a vista for her with endless development.

Another patient had a dream with many layers. Furry little animals, a wise infant grandson, red and white all over, third grade valentine post office upheaval, Queen's Croquet in *Alice*, red flush, white chill and yet nausea. It was all mixed up like this. Could anything be made of it? Yes.

It was a warning against being in a rush and compressing oneself. It is about a continual danger. It is about what makes for chaos. It makes for red flush and white chill and nausea. First impressions of a dream can seem to make no sense. Second impressions of a dream yield a perspective about not being in a hurry about just everything. It is best to wait for the unconscious to see what is really going on.

Could our patients find the right phrase of what was wrong with them far better than we can? Could such a phrase provide the pivot of what not to do and what to do? If we are alert to this possible originality of the patient, then we might have more patients leaving their sessions with us with a broad smile on their faces. They smile that they already knew what was wrong and how to set it right. They found the pivot they needed.

If we hear a word from a patient we have never heard before, we are probably close to delivering her or him to his or her second birth. I will provide two examples in which the patient's unconscious just came out with it.

One of my patients said offhand to me at the beginning of her session that she overthinks too much. Overthinks! I had never heard that word before. So I asked her what is overthinking? It was her original word for worrying. From her traumatic childhood in which she was badly abused, she was always on edge as an adult that she would get hurt more or she would hurt other people more.

She remarked that this was exhausting. How could she stop doing this to herself? I remarked back to her that it was very easy. She could not stop overthinking from popping into her mind, but she could change the subject. That would stop the positive feed back loop to overthinking. She loved it.

She had her pivot, from popping into it, and stepping out of it. Very nice work!

A second patient of mine remarked to me when we were making preparations for a video and my video man was popping in and out of the room that this was very striking. I replied that it was more like a movie studio than a clinical office. She retorted: *Where is the missing lion?* What? She explained that movie studios like MGM always started their films with a lion turning its head back and forth.

In the course of an hour, I said to her many times that she probably had never had a dream. She said that was right. Finally, she said she had one dream the night before seeing me. What was that? She dreamed that there was a murderer in a family. That of course made no sense to her, but I could probably explain it.

I did. She was about to marry into a family in which her fiancé's father was a member of the Lions' Club. He pretended to be an upstanding Lion, but actually he was always doing harm like trying to take custody of her fiancé's younger brother away from her good mother. She had found her missing lion that was a kind of murderer in the family.

Her unconscious apparently knew what her conscious did not want to admit. In five months she would be marrying into a family fraught with the dangers of injustice. She was shaken now. She felt rage at this Lion. She herself felt like a cowardly lion. She would like to be a brave lion and put this Lion into his place. She was very afraid she would lose control of her rage. She felt she must keep her cool in confronting the Lion.

In athletics so much depends on making a cool play. Say you are a second baseman. The shortstop fields a ground ball and you go to the second base to receive the toss and pivot in the air to throw out the batter at first base while simultaneously saving yourself from the slide of the runner coming into second base.

All of this sequence happens in a flash. It takes imagination like our patient needed to have to throw out the Lion while staying out of the way of his vicious slide. If you have never seen it performed, it is highly unlikely you will be able to pull if off. Pivots have to be practiced.

In our dream group every two weeks come forth the most startling creations one could never think of consciously. With permission to cite two examples from two of our members, I now proceed.

The first was of driving in a snowstorm. Strangely the dreamer was navigating by looking at all three rear view mirrors to stay on track with the past. Suddenly he pivoted to look forward and saw that he was driving right off the curving road and he crashed. Evidently the past was no guide to where things were going for him! That woke him up good!

As Cormac McCarthy (2017) wrote, the unconscious cares about two things, to warn about impending disasters and to imagine what has never been imagined before. This served both purposes. He needed to imagine that his road was not going to be like his past but curving in a new direction. How helpful!

The second was about swimming. Suddenly our dreamer imagined she could swoop into the air like a porpoise. Delighted, she did it over and over again. A related dream she had was of being asked to be a teacher but she did not know what to say. She had had many teachers, but she had not been one herself. She went to a group she was supposed to teach. The noise was deafening. Somehow she got the decibels lowered. In the quiet she could go into herself. I encouraged her. Waiting, her message rose up inside of her, quite like the porpoise inside of her rising into the air.

The two dreamers were being original in two different ways. Each of them was about to move in a different direction, not consciously, but unconsciously. The sieve of each was choosing a new way. As for Kekulé (McCarthy, 2017) dreaming of a snake swallowing itself by the tail to make a benzene ring, each of our dreamers was imagining a curve that had not existed before.

As for Poincaré (1910), a new proof might take start in a million places. He knew not which one would be fruitful for his proof of non-linear geometry.

So he waited. Several days later the starting point came to him from his sieve out of the night sea! Now he knew how to proceed, like our two dreamers knew for his or herself.

References

Alexander, F.: Dreams in pairs and series. *International Journal of Psychoanalysis* 1925, 6, 446–450.

Erikson, E.: The dream specimen of psychoanalysis. *Journal of the American Psychoanalytic Association* 1954, 2, 5–56.

Freud, S.: *Collected Works*, Volume IV. London: Hogarth Press, 1990.

Leveton, A.: The day residue. *International Journal of Psychoanalysis* 1961, 42, 506–516.

McCarthy, C.: The Kekulé problem. *Nautilus* (online), April 23, 2017.

Poincaré, H.: Mathematical creation. *The Monist* XX, July 3, 1910.

Stevenson, R.: *The Strange Case of Dr. Jekyll and Mr. Hyde* (1888). New York: Puffin Books, 1985.

Part IV
The Evolution Of The Species In Everyday Life

Chapter 10   How Our Species Came To Love Acceleration In Jumps

Chapter 11   Dangerous Intersections Of Evolution In Everyday Life

Chapter 12   Brakes Are Necessary If You Are To See The Whole Situation

10

How Our Species Came To Love Acceleration In Jumps

Your advantage in reading this chapter could be your being alert to your own rushing and accelerating all day long. Alert to your own rushing and accelerating, you can put on the brakes.

Our species has an undue faith in acceleration. Once it was fitting. Our species was disappearing in the Rift Valley in northeast Africa because of drought. Our numbers were probably less than one thousand, ninety thousand years ago and gradually becoming less. Then the rains came, and the vegetation flourished and thus the game also flourished. Now our species began its great breakout (Wilson, 2012). Small bands took small jumps perhaps twenty miles. There the farming and hunting were apt to be even better. One jump led to another for tens of thousands of years until our species dominated the entire planet.

The end of the Ice Age about ten thousand years ago led to the agricultural revolution of single crops such as rice and corn and wheat and barley. Huge surpluses arose. Now armies were needed to defend them and take them from other armies. Humanity needed specialists of all kinds. So they arose.

You can see this in North America. Arrivals from Europe settled on our east coast. Then a jump west began into the interior. One followed another until our species reached our west coast. More recently peoples from all over the world have arrived and followed suit in peopling our country.

In everyday life you can witness countless people rushing around without brakes. More is the byword. Rush is the action. Rush leads to heat. A thermodynamic revolution can be found almost everywhere. More rush, more

Part IV: The Evolution Of The Species

heat, more consuming, more garbage. Lévi-Strauss (1969) called these the hot engines, as opposed to the cold engines of the Ice Age that moved slowly within the yearly cycle.

One of my patients was typical. He was enthusiastic as a teacher to give one hundred and ten percent to his students. He exhausted himself. This was his 1st impression of his life. His 2nd impression was that this project was not sustainable. Neither was it a good example for his students! He thought: I must change my life. He did.

I had a super-annoying nightmare about this. I was being rushed between teaching two medical student groups. Someone said falsely that there are far less people in Door County in the summer time. I knew that was grossly false. I once lost my temper in swear words with a particular department chairman from the 1970s. This placed the dream when I was a young faculty member.

Also this situation was about far too much information acting as a piston upon myself as a doctor. Also this situation was about the flush chill illness brought about by the immense realm of the false.

How would you like to be subject to a piston pushing too much information and material upon you as a doctor? This is the chief illness of doctors. It brings about both a flush and a chill.

This night picture is an analogy like all dreams as 2nd impressions. The analogy points to the chief vulnerability of our species. It is mostly acceleration with far too little brakes. It is about more and more, faster and faster. When I imagine this piston, I can refuse to be bullied by it. I can go slowly.

I had a dream about an exchange with another doctor. I would see his patient in exchange for his soldering a delicate wire that has been severed. Everything is falling apart. Everything is multiplying: people, clothes and requests.

This is the illness of doctors and probably all of the helping professions. We are all beset with the information flood. It is that piston again pushing too much information and material upon us.

This is the 1st impression. The 2nd impression is this night painting of one to one exchanges. This remains possible. We can put the brakes on the acceleration of the information flood. Then there is room for a delicate exchange.

I had a primary care doctor for a patient. The doctor had felt jerked around much of every day in his practice. So many patients rushed him. Fix me now, they would insist. Or jump around in a flight of ideas. The doctor had to work very hard to insist on one idea at a time.

The doctor had a nightmare that woke him up. In the nightmare he was yet a student among students. The teacher told the students that they had to go buy a new pair of pants to bring back and sacrifice.

He began to run without thinking. If he could have put on the brakes, he would have imagined how preposterous was the demand of the teacher. He ran ten miles to a men's clothing store. When he arrived there he found the clerks all asleep in their beds. Should he run back to the teacher empty-handed?

He woke up. There and then, he decided to not run for anyone. He would listen to his 1st impression. He would not act. Acceleration would have little or no place in his practice. Of course, acceleration is called for when a place is on fire! That kind of emergency is infrequent.

Henceforth, he would note a patient's request and wait a while for his 2nd impression about what was being asked of him. Like General Kutuzov in Tolstoy's *War and Peace* (1869) who would listen to his Prussian generals with their absurd countless proposals to attack Napoleon, Kutuzov would nod his understanding and retire to his tent.

Not so easy, I am afraid. Somehow, despite his understanding, the doctor got rushed by his patients. Mondays seemed to sneak up on him and get to him. Patients came late and asked him for more than the allotted time. Coming near 5 PM was the worst.

Opioid prescriptions for chronic pain seemed to be called for just when the clinic was going to close for the day. On 1st impression, the need seemed to be valid. But, really, he knew so little about the patient. He would tell his nurse to set up the prescription so he could sign off on it. He was so vulnerable to pleas of chronic pain.

By four in the morning, he would wake up thinking that he would not do much about the chronic pain. Its validity might be so and might not be so. He would need to take weeks to arrive at a 2nd impression about the patient's whole life. At four in the morning, accelerating music ran on faster and faster in him. Such acceleration distorts sound decisions.

He found himself in the throes of his species to do more and more, based on knowing less and less the faster he practiced. Calm needs to be waited for. Not to be compressed needs also to be waited for. It was up to him to slow down, despite the urging of the patients. He would think about what they asked for, later.

Not only are we vulnerable to rushing and acceleration, but also our world is equally vulnerable to rushing and acceleration. The terrible fire in Notre Dame de Paris seemed to be totally unexpected. One of my patients showed me his beautiful video taken in the nave last December, and now it is all gone.

It was unexpected if you did not know that the roof and spire and attic were made out of wood ever getting more dried out and flammable. The slightest flame was all it took. How fast fires can take off into catastrophe! So quickly it was a ball of fire!

We are prone to imagine our worlds as secure. Riding in our cars can become suddenly vulnerable to drivers in a tremendous hurry. Stop signs and yellow and red lights they can ignore at any time. We can become their victims. In my practice I have a number of patients whose lives were suddenly ruined like this.

Is health guaranteed? I think not. Friends in good shape suddenly can't play tennis any more. Some illness and they might be dead.

Is there a moral to this story? I suppose it is to be grateful that things are going well and alert to sudden changes. One can have an eye out for known unknowns, such as I have just enumerated. The unknown unknowns are just going to happen from time to time. We will have had no idea that such could happen, as such the nearly complete destruction of Notre Dame de Paris. I had no idea that one was possible. There is a lot we do not know. I will not forget this one.

On context everything depends. For example, listening to beautiful and original music from the Berlin Philharmonic Orchestra with your spouse for one evening is happiness. Will it last? Try to make it!

Will the unconscious allow this? Try to make it! Evidently the unconscious considers this to be dangerous. For example, I had a nightmare that I was playing hockey for the University of Wisconsin against the University of Minnesota. I was recklessly moving the puck in an unorthodox way that baffled my opponents so I scored three goals and we won.

I found several of their big players surrounding me. I was doomed. Hockey is a game of robbery. Steal the puck from the opponents and get it past their goalie! Evidently this must be carried out by the rules on a noble playing field. Evidently my huge opponents felt I had cheated. Evidently they were going to kill me. I had to wake up to save my life.

Notice we come here to another vulnerability of our species! The males of Homo sapiens are about as violent as male chimpanzees. Kill or be killed!

The females of Homo sapiens have a different vulnerability. My wife had a different nightmare the same night as my treacherous hockey game. Her nightmare was of being at a country club where she did not belong. She felt flush chilled and nauseated and took much of the next day to recover. Belong or be cast out!

Almost always, hurrying to be helpful from a hysterical 1st impression gets you in trouble. Brakes or acceleration are apt to be mistaken. Waiting for a 2nd impression you can come to a better option and you can pivot to it.

I had a patient who went to a retreat where the retreat director rushed to her quarters with a pale face. "You have lice! The massage therapist saw them!"

By taking this to be the certain truth, my patient flew into a panic. After some while, she got a grip on herself and asked a doctor friend to have a close look. After fifteen minutes of examination, the diagnosis was no lice. What relief! How much better for her it would have been to take the 1st impression as maybe yes, maybe no! She was too quickly persuaded. She was too nice.

I had another patient who was also too nice in a different way that made him ill. As a principal he received many reports that a certain teacher was deranged. For each report he met with the teacher. He was carefully matter of fact, but the result was always rage in his face from the teacher.

Why did he keep taking this craziness? He had some kind of attitude and practice of giving the benefit of the doubt. I asked him how many times he should suffer this before he fired the teacher?

It turned out that he had a big sister crazy like this. His mother always insisted that he be kind. His mother always insisted that his sister was troubled and deserved his endless patience. He dared not disobey his mother. Thus was he ruled?

I saw him every several months for several years. Perhaps he was finally persuaded that every meeting with this crazy teacher made him seriously ill. He need not sacrifice himself. He fired the teacher instead of rushing to the rescue of this poor soul.

This is a common fate of teachers, doctors, ministers and just about every profession, not to mention spouses and children. David Malan (1976) called it the helping profession syndrome. I call it being too damned nice. Half the world acts this out, at least. Accelerating to the rescue is very hazardous to the rescuer, like drowning as a lifeguard. It is a weakness of our species.

Nice people tend to be swamped like Dr. Jekyll (Stevenson, 1886). Everyone else's problem becomes theirs. Not only that, they are loaded with information. Are you going to expect anything from them? Is there any room? Doubt it!

Given this has become their nature, their devotion and their rushing from one thing to another, I recalibrate what to expect of them. This is that I expect nothing. Every now and then, I am pleasantly surprised that they show up.

What is recalibration? Of course there are many kinds for all our instruments. Being oriented is the one I am talking about. It means re-measuring what to expect from someone, like how much. Will it keep you from being jarred? Well yes, when you are never disappointed, and on occasion, pleasantly surprised.

References

Lévi-Strauss, C.: *Conversations with Lévi-Strauss*. London: Jonathan Cape, 1969.

Malan, D.: *The Frontier of Brief Psychotherapy*. New York: Plenum, 1976.

Stevenson, R.: *The Strange Case of Dr. Jekyll and Mr. Hyde* (1886). New York: Puffin Books, 1985.

Tolstoy, L.: *War and Peace* (1869). New York: W.W. Norton, 1966.

Wilson, E.: *The Social Conquest of Earth*. New York: Liveright, 2012.

11

Dangerous Intersections Of Evolution In Everyday Life

Your advantage in reading this chapter might well be the advantage of saving your life.

Stoplights are instructive. Yellow lights seem to trigger acceleration rather than brakes in some drivers. Red lights seem to do this also. It is not difficult to get struck in the intersection from the side or from behind.

I discussed this with a medical student. He told me he could not afford to be late. I replied that he could not afford to be dead. This was a 2nd impression for him that got his attention.

Stuart Jones and I have been conducting lecture discussions with our resident candidates for the last several years in the last hour of their two-day visits to our department. We seem to elicit their full attention and eloquence. We pose pictures of the situations where the greatest dangers and opportunities lie for them and their patients. Almost always they have already encountered these things full force as medical students.

I suggest to them that linear psychiatry is easy. A little more medication or less is simply a matter of trial and error. What is not easy and not usually taught is when linear psychiatry suddenly turns into non-linear psychiatry. We have decided on five pictures for them as the most important to understand.

The first is called the Lotka Scenario that many biologists call "the engine of evolution." All animals have to forage, like the little voles on the prairie. If the voles remain secure in their burrows, there will be no more voles for the lack of sustenance. If the voles foray for their vital grain, there is a great danger that the red tail hawks and wolves will be waiting to take them for their sustenance.

The voles need to hesitate at their 1st impression. The coast seems clear to get their precious grain. This impression may be wrong. They need to take a 2nd impression of whether red tail hawks are circling above them or wolves sneaking up along the ground.

The voles that continue to evolve are those that are not in a hurry. They need a double description. They need to sight the potential grain. They also need to sight the predators. They must not be completely cautious. They also must not be too rash. They must not get too far from their secure burrows. They must beat the predator back to their burrows and dive into them for their safety.

Our resident candidates get the analogy to their own predicament and those of their patients. There is a balance between somewhere between green light and red light. Even so in their visits to our department! It may be an opportunity to get what they need, but it also may risk getting hurt. All foraging is like this. Finding a mate is like this. Finding friends is like this. Finding recognition for being a good medical student or resident is like this. All of these things are intersections, for being well or ill.

The second picture is of the catastrophe theory of René Thom (1972). The x-axis of this graph is the amount of stimulation. The y-axis is of the amount of response. There tends to be a little more response with more stimulation. This is linear psychiatry, such as more medication for more distress.

The sequence that follows is the most important one in psychiatry. At a certain point of stimulation, one more step in the stimulation reaches what Thom called the catastrophe point. Suddenly the response is totally non-linear, an explosion like rage or mania or psychosis, and/or an implosion of depression.

This tends to catch us unawares. Things were getting worse slowly. Suddenly, things are totally dangerous. The patient just could not bear any more. Our candidates often remind us that metals under strain act like this or liquids being heated going into a boil. Our candidates often remind us that many patients have little awareness of the state of their bodies, so they do not know themselves that the slightest irritation to Dr. Jekyll will have Mr. Hyde running over anyone in his way. It is not just patients that do this, but also doctors! Of course, anyone out of touch with his or her body will have this vulnerability.

Naturally our discussions tend at this point to ask how losing it like this could be prevented. The usual answer is that mindfulness can slow down and take in what tensions are already in the body. For example, worriers almost always build up tensions in their neck and shoulders. If they can be taught to look to the state of their necks and shoulders, they can sometimes slow down.

Others register tension in their gastrointestinal organs. Others get flushed or chilled or both. Others get headaches. Others get fibromyalgia. There is no end to the list of places where tension is registered.

The third picture naturally follows from this second picture. The third picture is of a doctor beset with twenty sources of information on every patient. He or she is squeezed to the point of explosion or implosion or both.

Indeed, a common tendency with a huge agenda like this is to run faster. Huge agendas make people crazy. It is like skating on thin ice.

The only remedy for an impending catastrophe is to step on the brake and step back and consider making things simpler. This may yield a 2nd impression, such as limiting the sources of information to a few privileged ones that are known to be reliable. You can't afford to listen to many of them.

The fourth picture is the hazards of intersections. These are likely places to get killed or badly injured. A sensible remedy is to practice taking yellow lights as time to brake and not accelerate. If you have such a discipline, you had better also stay alert to how closely the cars or trucks are behind you and pull over if they insist on driving right into your trunk! You also need to stay alert about cars and trucks flying through the intersections from right or left on yellow lights and even red lights.

I have seen many patients whose bodies and lives have been ruined by this craziness. Getting mad at it often makes it worse. Yelling at it or giving it the finger or fist is apt to agitate the furious driver into worse behavior.

The fifth picture for our candidates is the one of having 2nd impressions every night that we call dreams or nightmares. We may not like what they have to picture, but these pictures are our friends and teachers.

Getting up in a hurry in the morning to rush into the day robs yourself. Unfortunately most people are on the fly with their huge agendas when their alarms wakes them. That is the huge vulnerability of our species.

There are many more dangerous intersections worth mentioning. A rule of thumb that keeps coming to my mind is stairs, fires and cars. One shape swallows another. Another great text is that of Verdi's *Requiem* (1874). The mass is about saving us on the day of fire and final judgment. Not to throw us into hell forever. It is all about being in the light of God, and not cast into the dark. The final solo of the soprano is the most moving. Her cry is "Libera me!"

I want to mention three other intersections of life and death that matter. One I discovered the other dark night. Moving from bright light into dim light is treacherous. Afro-Americans have had almost no security. Six million fled from the south to the north, finding it only a little better. I noticed this the other dark night. I was going down our stairs, noticing it is best to make four points of contact, hands and feet, lifting one off at a time. Such caution on stairs in the dark is worth taking if you possibly can.

There are patients whose energies are harmful. It is best not to intersect with them. Often they are making impossible demands. For example, I had a new patient come to me complaining that her new primary care provider would not prescribe massive opioids for her unbearable pain and benzodiazepines for her anxiety and panic attacks. I replied that no doctor would be willing to do this because of dangerous possible fatal respiratory suppression. She retorted that her previous primary care doctor did prescribe the two drugs and that was perfect for her.

I hoped that was all I would see of her. By no means! She came back saying the same thing over and over again. I told her I agreed with the primary care doctor that it would be malpractice to keep on with the benzodiazepines. This did not stop her getting more and more loud as I ushered her out of my office.

Actually, I needed some time to calm down from being shrieked at. I did calm down. Then I had a second impression that an SSRI (serotonin selective reuptake inhibitor) would be the first line of treatment for panic attacks anyway. I hoped the primary care provider would be willing to do it. Thankfully, she was willing.

That night I had a nightmare of being swamped and drowned by a screaming patient. This 2nd impression was very helpful to me. I was quite clear with myself that I am not willing to sacrifice myself to this kind of life saving. Some intersections of energies are fatal to the lifeguard in the hands of such a malignant swimmer. There are plenty of these malignant swimmers screaming for help. It is best to step back before you dive in. I know too many doctors that jump in without thinking.

Originality tends to be a problem with conventionality. I had a patient who had a nightmare about this. He dreamed of trying to stay neutral at a celebration of his alma mater by swimming at a ninety-degree angle. Any original contribution got attacked violently by the conventionality. The perpendicular swim might go unnoticed and thus unharmed.

Reference

Thom, R.: *Structural Stability and Morphogenesis* (1972). Boulder, Colorado: Westview Press, 1988.

12

Brakes Are Necessary If You Are To See The Whole Situation

Your advantage in reading this chapter could be that you decide to limit the amount of information you take in. With too much information you cannot think.

Brakes are under-developed in our species. Huge agendas guarantee exhaustion, as our resident candidates tell us. On the other hand, doing too little can result in failure to impress. Our resident candidates know this too.

As I said in the last chapter, Stuart Jones and I give a seminar in the last hour of visits from resident candidates to our department. We show them drawings of the dangers they need to be ready for. Paulo Freire called this method of education problem posing for peasants in Brazil in his book *Pedagogy of the Oppressed* (1970). They find their own generative and fresh words for what they see. The drawing that strikes our resident candidates the most is the drawing of a doctor being compressed from all sides by far too many sources of information for every patient. The doctor looks like he is going to explode like a rocket.

If they and we are going to last, they and we need to choose which information channels are the most relevant and set aside the information channels that are not absolutely necessary. Then calm can prevail.

Here is how I avoided a typical blunder from concluding too soon. I had a patient, a young woman who had made two suicide attempts. The second resulted in being in a coma for two days. Her mother brought her in to see me. After a brief hospitalization in psychiatry, she had come home and did nothing but stay in bed. The young woman seemed almost catatonic. She sat straight up and said almost nothing. She was oriented to place and date and time.

The mother knew that another suicide attempt might happen. I said it was time to take her to the emergency room. The mother was grateful I knew how grave the situation was. She agreed to take her daughter to the emergency room.

The next day I found out that the daughter had refused to go to the emergency room. I felt helpless to help mother and daughter. That was my 1st impression.

I did not give up. I called the mother four days in a row and she did not answer. I had no idea what was happening.

On the fourth day, the mother finally called me back. She told me that things were better. She had told her daughter, as we had recommended, that continuing to stay in bed and doing nothing was just going to make her worse and worse. The mother told her daughter that she would call the police if the daughter did not get out of bed and eat and shower and take her medicines. The daughter was angry. The mother replied that the mother's job was to call a halt to the daughter furthering her own regression.

The daughter got out of bed and ate and showered and took her medicines! This mother had known instinctively what to do, but my backing her instincts was very helpful to her and she was very grateful to me.

I had not acceded to my 1st impression that the case was impossible. I had not known that the mother could supply the force needed. Knowing that I did not know left room for a better outcome. I had not been in a hurry. I had used my brakes and finally got a full view of the whole situation.

Getting a new iPhone in place of my old smart phone was a very strange experience. You have these intense professional electronic fusions with young Apple people asking you one hundred questions. They pour in the answers to you to make the phone work. One missing letter? It won't work.

You have to depend upon them intensively. But you really are not close. You really do not see their shadows. All you see is their drilled performance they have made hundreds of times. They have to act with very good manners to grasping clients. I do not envy them. They have to have very good brakes to see and tolerate the whole situation.

Most professions require this kind of patience. While the Apple agent was working hard to help me with my iPhone, a lady across the table kept interrupting us. I know just how the agent feels when I am being a doctor. So many patients feel entitled to interrupt like this.

I have learned to cope with such questions. I say I will think about the question that I cannot answer on 1st impression. I will wait for my 2nd impression. Thus I do not allow myself to be rushed. I would be ill if I allowed it. Brakes are so crucial in a world of accelerating patients.

Too much of everything has become the rule in this society. Yuja Wang is a great pianist but she wears out her body in giving too many concerts. This got into me. I dreamed of a famous fly-fishing river whose banks were crowded with fishermen. This was like too much of cities, airports, highways, information, forms to fill out for the veteran's hospital and fifty pages on opioids to study to renew my license. In this society there are hardly any brakes.

I have learned to look at my 1st impressions of these excessive situations and wait for my 2nd impressions for how to do as little as possible. Not to make myself ill is my aim.

From a very different angle, I found the importance of our being mammals. In a very cold and immense universe, we mammals have to find our warm burrows. In such warm burrows, we find our comfort. At the farm of a friend, I noticed his new hot tub. Going for lunch at La Baguette and then for beer at my favorite store, I noticed a very friendly and warm respect.

For us mammals, life is unbearable without being welcomed where we go. When we are warmly welcomed, we feel we are in the right world. If we meet coldness and harshness, we know we can only bear so much of it. If we meet such cold and harsh intersections, we also now we must be sparing of dealing it out to others. When we see the effects of coldness and harshness dealt by ourselves, we become more merciful. We shudder at what King Lear did to Cordelia, and what Goneril and Regan did to him.

When King Lear fled into the unbearable cold and stormy night, his only company was the Fool. When King Lear's heart broke, so broke the Fool's heart. Shakespeare knew how to show us what is unbearable for us.

King Lear had no brakes on his demands for praise from his three daughters. Cordelia replied that she loved him as her duty. Goneril and Regan pumped out lies him about their enormous admiration of him.

By this route, King Lear warmly put himself into the hands of his cold and cruel daughters. By this route, King Lear put himself into their net. May we never be so foolish ourselves! May we never force our children or really anyone to tell us how great we are! We will either get lies back or our listeners fleeing from us.

Strangely, I had a dream at midnight of selling five hundred copies of this book in one day. Literally, it could not be so. An analogy it could be. I decided to stay calm. Towards morning, I dreamed of sticky flypaper, endless obsessional tangles.

By morning, I had a 2nd impression that made sense. I am to put on the brakes against too much information. Too much information is harmful. Rather, it is far better to keep one's decks clear so that strong lines of development can stand out.

Are there patients that will flood you? For sure! For example, I saw a young man for a first visit that would never stop talking. For any question I posed to him, he could talk all day, he himself said. As he said, he was the perfect salesman of anything and he had been. Abrupt transitions, as Sullivan (1956) would say are the only remedy.

Getting mad was not going to help me. The information flood he prided himself on. After I asked him any question, the floodgates were open to his salesmanship. A smooth transition of explaining why I was going to another subject he would simply ignore to resume his sales pitch. A sharper accepted transition would not faze him either.

Rather I would simply go to another subject after I got a sentence or two that would otherwise continue non-stop. I did not get mad. I just got even. We were just going somewhere else as a matter of fact.

Curiously this got me finished with him in an hour. The horse just let me change the subject and direction perhaps one hundred times. Did I like it? No! It was just my only way out. The interviewer has to take charge with such salesmen or he or she will be sorry.

I had another and perhaps a more important discovery of information flood calling for brakes. I read to my wife one evening how Henry Beston (1928) in one paragraph could make use of declarative, exclamatory, imperative and interrogative sentences to be totally present to the different sounds of the surf on the great beach of Cape Cod. Music with absolutely clear sentences was what it was. My wife chose Rachmaninoff's *2nd Symphony* that did much the same.

What was going to wake me up at 3 AM? On this Friday into Saturday night, I was already dreading like I do on Sunday into Monday night my medical practice to come. On Monday I would get back a patient from the inpatient service that has nothing to go on for herself. I would be expected to change her mood so she could do something besides waste all her time. On Sunday, I would be the faculty backup for the emergency room for twenty-four hours and to make rounds in the hospital mostly to attend to just such these trivial cases. Behaviorism is supposed to fix such things.

Don't wake up angry like this! Is the Lotka Scenario not about taking what is good for you and refusing to swallow what is bad for you? Is it not about keeping your decks clear of entropy? I felt disgust and anger.

Going up to my study, in bright light, I found myself shocked by all the papers I had tacked to my white walls over nearly the last forty years. Leaving a few of importance to me, I began to pull down most of them. Most of them were things of the past that no longer matter to me.

One was very important, by Daisetz Suzuki, page 361 of his *Zen and Japanese Culture* (1938). Suzuki wrote that nature was about lines of movement. Also he wrote that identity is a static condition that is decidedly associated with death. Also he wrote that clearing away of all conceptual scaffolds is imperative.

Also I noticed that many of my drawings had far too much detail on them. This is like bad music. I decided to retain the drawings that had a few beautiful lines of movement like we find in Beston's prose and in Rachmaninoff's *2nd Symphony*.

Are my decks not clear now? Will this not make space and time for beautiful movements to come forth? Clear your decks for just this! I still have quite a few tacks to take off my walls.

Are not all these examples in this chapter a version of the same thing, of way too much, with no coherent lines of movement? Exhaust yourself! This is how to wear out as fast as possible. Always accelerate! Jump from one tangent to another! You will not know who you are or what you are. Just pile up things! You will not have any time to think. You will not have any line of development for yourself. You will be quite busy. You will know many other people just like yourself. Actually you will hardly know them at all. This context is the diagnosis of your illness. Nothing else is possible when the context is racing around. I say this to indicate something much better is possible.

Is there a simpler way to explain the lack of brakes in us, in our species? Canetti (1984) did it in *Crowds and Power* in 1960 in German and won the Nobel Prize for it. Iris Murdoch the novelist knew about it and said this (Gary Simoneau, personal communication): "The traditional novel, you cannot avoid being funny, because human life is funny. Any prolonged description produces something funny and places where the thing is absurd."

Canetti described human life as organized in packs, like the hunting pack, the war pack, the lamenting pack and the increase pack. The first three of the four are what they say. The strange one is the increase pack. As Murdoch said, prolonged descriptions produce something funny and places where the thing is absurd.

Would you think that we could be sucked into packs that increase in numbers just for the sake of increasing? Strange to say, we are most

Part IV: The Evolution Of The Species

vulnerable to this pack formation. Canetti thought it was driven by desperation in the Ice Age. For example, a Plains Indian Tribe depended on hunting the buffalo. If the buffalo were not sighted for weeks, they put on buffalo garb and danced without cessation until the buffalo came. They became the buffalo that attracted the buffalo by their frenetic dancing.

In the twentieth century, as in World War I and in World War II, this is what happened. Millions died in joining up that they could not resist. It fed the totalitarian killers like Stalin and Hitler.

Now it is legion but mostly banal. Nearly everyone is caught up in an increase pack of increasing something. Increasing the sales of anything! Increasing the score of teams! Increasing the votes for candidates! Increasing your salary! Increasing your number of papers written for prestigious journals!

Is it a killer like the packs of Stalin and Hitler? No one is murdered. Rather what happens is that the increase of numbers runs away from what is being present and being beautiful? Yes. My wife was recently in Washington, DC for a few days with two old college friends in a hotel where the real estate people were having a conference for five days. They were bent on learning how to sell more properties. That might not kill you, but it might rob you of caring about what is beautiful: numbers, not presence.

Oh this vulnerability of our species! Rushing and accelerating! For two nights in a row, did I have to be woken at 3 AM by my sieve? Apparently I needed it. The first night I was reminded of my double take about Kamala Harris taking apart Joe Biden in the first Democratic Party debate. She did it beautifully, but I was alarmed by her charismatic style. Martin Luther King has this charismatic style and made serious objections like Kamala and got shot on a balcony and died for it. I feared for her.

Did I have to be woken again the next night at 3 AM? Apparently, yes! I take it on faith when I am woken like this. This time it was I, not Kamala, who was attempting too much, too fast and at the last minute. I was having supper at one table and had to have some of my wife's supper at another table. I had organized two tennis doubles matches back to back and reserved the courts. I had organized a panel of four of us on cancer patients and their families at 7 PM (I used to do this sort of thing). A certain guy was mocking me for attempting too much. I felt like I was the epitome of the Democratic Party. Attempt everything at once to solve the nation's problems, fighting each other, while failing to defeat Trump with a single decisive promise, like raising wages a couple of dollars to everyone. Do I not deserve to be woken up for failing the country in the next election? Yes.

References

Beston, H.: *The Outermost House, A Year on the Great Beach of Cape Cod* (1928). New York: St. Martin's Griffin, 1988.

Canetti, E.: *Crowds and Power*. New York: Farrar, Straus and Giroux, 1984.

Freire, P.: *Pedagogy of the Oppressed*. New York: Herder and Herder, 1970.

Sullivan, H.: *Clinical Studies in Psychiatry* (1956). New York: W.W. Norton, 1976.

Suzuki, D.: *Zen and Japanese Culture* (1938). Princeton, New Jersey: Princeton University Press, 1959.

The Great World In Everyday Life

Chapter 13   The Immense Realm Of The False

Chapter 14   Noble Playing Fields

Chapter 15   Religious Deliverance: Light And Dark

13

The Immense Realm Of The False

Your advantage in reading this chapter might well be the hardest one to swallow. If you could swallow it, you could save yourself a lot of grief. You would be less conventional, but perhaps you could be happier.

The phrase of this title was a phrase of Pietro Citati in his book, *Tolstoy* (1986). Citati thought it apt for each of Tolstoy's great novels, *War and Peace* (1869) and *Anna Karenina* (1878), because most of the characters were putting on performances that were extremely misleading. In Chapter 4, I called them life lies as Ibsen would say. Pierre in the first novel and Levin in the second novel fell for most of them. They were captured countless times because of their naivete in trusting 1st impressions. Their education came slowly, as they slowly learned to step back and wait for 2nd impressions to get closer to the truth.

Another famous example of naivete was the character Candide being misled by his teacher Pangloss to get beat up everywhere they went in Voltaire's novel *Candide* (1759). Yet another was Don Quijote in Cervantes' novel *Don Quijote* (1605).

Little has changed. Almost all of advertising and politics are smiling faces full of promises that are not entirely true. Marx (1867) called it commodity fetishism. Such things are supposed to save your life. This is highly doubtful. You might get a headache instead.

One of my patients was typical. Her husband died young. This left her lonely indeed. She was persuaded that making new girl friends was just what she needed. It mostly turned out that these so-called friends were swamped with their own troubles and thus had no time for her.

I am like everyone else. I trusted 1st impressions for many decades until I saw for myself that they were misleading. For example, I fell for an ad about washing my Apple computer for $300. I thought I must need it. Fortunately, my credit card was not working! I just closed the connection to these opportunistic devils.

A month or two later I had a nightmare that I was still falling for the fraud! Did I not learn my lesson? My unconscious knew I was still vulnerable to the likes of this foolishness. It threw me back into the 1960s and 1970s when I was on the staff of group relations conferences. My colleagues acted as if Bion (1959) knew everything about group dynamics. Groups they thought always acted as if one. I published a series of papers about the importance of steering between subgroups so each had its say and something original could emerge. My colleagues were enraged with me at their scientific meeting. That violent attack woke me up. My 2nd impression of them was no longer naive. I left the field. They definitely felt they owned it.

A similar naivete was in charge of me for all of the 1980s in the field of brief dynamic psychotherapy (Gustafson, 1986, *The Complex Secret of Brief Psychotherapy*). It took me ten years before I woke up. Malan and Davanloo and Michels were ferocious. They wanted no such complex secret. Their followers were similar in their rage with me. They just insisted on following these gods and telling me to shut up. How many attacks did I need to be ready for the next attack? I needed ten years, evidently. The immense realm of the false is a director culture (Freire, 1970) that is extremely dogmatic. Opposing them is futile.

A subtler realm of the false comes from what John Gedo (1979) (Gustafson, 1986, Chapter 9) called *The Hierarchy of Personal Aims*. Gedo illustrated this confusion regarding *A Case of Toulouse Lautrec*.

His patient was a full time graduate student who also worked full time for the university while he threw himself full time into saving his girlfriend. Three full time projects got in each other's way. He also dressed flagrantly like Toulouse Lautrec. Gedo told him that his life would be a mess until he could decide what came ahead of what.

I have encountered versions of this in most of our patients. Their agendas are huge and impossible to fulfill. As Gedo said to his patient, I have said to my patients: "You do not even have time to see me to figure out what comes ahead of what. You need to see me regularly to sort out your priorities."

In other words, most of our patients are so heavily freighted by lists of burdens that they lose track of what they care about most. Mothers and fathers once had had an image of bringing up children. Now this image is lost in rushing around from one obligation to another.

The Immense Realm Of The False

Citati illustrates this over and over in Tolstoy's two great novels. For example, Prince Bolkonsky in *War and Peace* believed in rationality over all else. This precision like clockwork is what he practiced.

He was like the German generals who thought you could plan battles by some abstraction. In reality, the battles could not be commanded. The action consisted of masses of confusion, advancing parts and retreating parts that no one was in control of.

Prince Andrei was his son. He too sought to control everything. He did not wake up until he was shelled and lay dying on the battlefield of Austerlitz. He found himself looking up at a vast sky. This moved him. All these pretenses of controlling battles were absurd. Too many forces on both sides could not be anticipated. The two sides came rushing at each other and no one could see what was happening in all the smoke.

This is what happens to most of our patients. They are totally confused by their own days that are really not their own, just rushing from one thing to another. Perhaps it is more precise to say that things rush them this way and that. This is our so-called epidemic of attention deficit hyperactivity disorder (ADHD). I call it the tangential mind. Captives of it start out in one direction and are compelled to rush to another and then another and another until they cannot remember what they started. One patient described her life to me as a huge collection of post-its. One such reminder gets a hold of her and then she is captured by another post-it reminder and then another and another. She said she ends up doing many things that are not important and forgets what is most important.

Notice that acceleration makes this go. Our evolution demonstrated in Part IV is about how this acceleration operates in everyday life. The etymology of false is from the Old French *faux*, or *fallere*, to deceive. It is nearly everywhere.

It seems to me that acceleration operates in everyday life as information overload. This is called teaching. It is didacticism. Bad teachers flood their pupils with information.

Play is what I love the most. You cannot play at anything if there is too much in your head. It moves instinctively, bottom up. It cannot be thinking. That is why my tennis coach Jim Shirley only shows me one thing I might do differently at a time.

More is better? I doubt it. Runaway generators of more details have one virtue, keeping people busy, as in more worries, more information, more documentation, more garbage, more addiction and more promotions. You lose any picture you might had of what is beautiful and holy and kind.

McGilchrist wrote a book about this called *The Master and His Emissary* (2009). He argued that the right brain is the master for imagining whole situations. The left-brain can focus on details like a servant or emissary.

If the left-brain betrays and usurps the master, all is lost. Everyone becomes a salesperson of one commodity or another. This is our immense realm of the false. If we see how this works, we can put on the brakes. We can wait to see what would be worthwhile for us.

Dreams on Sunday night into Monday tend to show sharply what is wrong at the workplace. Is it not better to be ready?

Can friends be helpful about this to us with their own dreams? Absolutely. One friend dreamed of a vast white empty hall. He told me that he used to be naive about working for a corporation. Now with this picture of business to strengthen his conviction, however nice their manners, he can see how impersonal it really is. Can you not be let go at any time? Is that not downright impersonal? You bet.

Can we help ourselves directly from our own night painting on Sunday night into Monday morning? Absolutely! I had a pair of such night paintings about 4 AM.

The first was about my father the businessman. He was writing out a number in five digits like 10876. He was doing business on five deals at once. He was promising to cook a five-course supper for my wife and me. When I woke up, I doubted he would.

The second night picture of the pair was about a vast area of tracts of lands on which to build new houses at the edge of a beautiful rolling county. It was supposed to be a good business deal. When I woke up, I doubted this would be a good idea. Yes, it might bring a lot of money to the seller selling all these lots. Buying one, on the other hand, would be altogether impersonal. Pretty soon more and more tracts would be sold. These would no place to situate oneself and a family. The same kind of houses would be seen as far as the horizon.

As I wrote in my Preface, night paintings or pictures can pose problems to think about from these 2nd impressions. The immense realm of the false, nowadays, is about absolutely impersonal deals. Consider our politics! Consider our advertising! Consider our educations!

As for summing it up, I had another Hamlet dream, such as I have had on and off for a very long time. I dreamed I was the producer and director of a comedy to be played in the University Theatre. Everything was set up, the actors and the stage set but for one last thing I had to go get in a taxi before we began. When I got back, the play had been called off, supposedly because of two little torches that were not allowed. Who did not allow two little torches in the University Theatre? What? I never heard of that! A guy named George Doak was in charge of the University Theatre. He said I could definitely put on my play next year.

What made this a Hamlet play within a play? It was simply because my play obviously alarmed Claudius who called it off and fled. Our Claudius is Trump who has murdered his sister Hilary Clinton and taken away for himself what belonged rightfully to Hilary as President. This puts us in Elsinore where everything beautiful has gone rotten. I cannot do a damn thing about it. That sums up our politics. It is our immense realm of the false. I am for doing what I can on a very small stage like our department.

Would my unconscious stop about that? No, it would not. The large political stage refuses to go away. I dream we are very happy when suddenly we undergo a massive aerial attack exploding with light overhead like a thunderstorm. The Nazi officers come in to take over our house for storing their records on each other in medical charts. Their apparent leader, an evil marshal in a white coat with an evil face is but ten yards outside our cabin looking like he is in a panic.

This reminds me of the Hamlet dream the night before of Claudius in a panic despite his seeming to have taken over Elsinore and his seeming to have a grip on everyone but Hamlet himself. I take this to be an analogy or metaphor for picturing the state of Trump or Trumpistan. No one knows what extreme thing he might do if his panic takes him over altogether. My unconscious knows that nobody knows. We will try to live well in our small little world despite this craziness on the world scale.

References

Bion, W.: *Experiences in Groups*. New York: Basic Books, 1959.

Citati, P.: *Tolstoy*. New York: Shocken, 1986.

Freire, P.: *Pedagogy of the Oppressed*. New York: Herder and Herder, 1970.

Gedo, J.: *Beyond Interpretation, Toward A Revised Theory for Psychoanalysis*. New York: International Universities Press, 1979.

Gustafson, J.: *The Complex Secret of Brief Psychotherapy*. New York: W.W. Norton, 1986.

Marx, K.: *Capital, Critique of Political Economy* (in German). Verlag von Otto Meisner, Hamburg, 1867.

McGilchrist, I.: *The Master and His Emissary*. New Haven: Yale University Press, 2009.

14

Noble Playing Fields

Your advantage in reading this chapter could be the happiest. Having play all your life could be the greatest gift to yourself. It could spare you much drudgery. It could orient you to find companions on noble play fields. Your opinion of the potential of human beings could rise.

Johann Huizinga was the author of this subject in his great book, *Homo Ludens* (1938) that means humanity the playing animal. This animal knows how to set context markers for places where contests are to be played out. The contestants instinctively know how to play fairly and generously. Dogs know how to do this and so do bears.

Huizinga was very clear about the limits of such playing fields. Beyond their context markers, almost anything can happen. Even within them, there is a danger of piling up rules upon rules that act as rank layers that deaden the players.

Huizinga also knew in 1938 that the Germans were coming into Holland soon with ferocious intent. He was taken prisoner as a notable professor and put in prison and died in 1944.

I knew a young man who loved noble playing fields conducted well. He went to college and tried out for the basketball team. He made the freshman team as a starter, but was sorely disappointed. The coach was a screamer.

Any mistake you made you would get yelled at and often jerked out of the game by this screaming coach. All five of the team continually looked over their shoulders at the bench and could not feel free to play. They were tight.

Then a fortunate thing happened. The assistant coach was put in charge for one game. He was a real player and let his five move instinctively. They did. It was beautiful to watch.

My friend actually broke his ankle in the second overtime and went back to the fraternity house only to be woken up with all of the other pledges to be rushed down the stairs by the so-called brothers at midnight with bells clanging and bright lights in their faces. This was the announcement of Hell Week where the pledges had to work night and day for a week. My friend forgot to telephone the regular coach and got kicked off the time for insubordination. This was very painful.

Noble playing fields are vulnerable.

I had a patient who had a pair of dreams at 3 AM. The first of the pair was about what he did not want to happen, that is, to be finished. The second of the pair was about what he did want to happen, that is, to keep evolving. They looked about the same as in Robert Frost's (1920) poem, *The Road Less Taken*.

The first of the dreams was about returning to Boston where he found Back Bay covered with a dead brown lid. You could walk across it from Boston to Cambridge but everything was the same and it was all over.

The second of the dreams was about getting to Cambridge and buying a copy of Heidegger's *An Introduction to Metaphysics* (1959) from the Mandrake Book Store. The color was also brown, but this brown made all the difference. It was about Heidegger's distinction between things that were finished and things that would ever keep developing in beautiful play between opposites.

The mandrake is a root to promote conception. This is what the owner of the Mandrake Book Store desired. He knew what Frost knew about two paths diverging in a yellow wood, one fatal and one beautiful and fertile.

There are great worlds that are not false but rather noble (Snow, 1994). The vertical shines forth in nobility and in the sacred. Our house has four copies of Vermeer paintings. His light could be seen as noble and sacred.

Thoreau is well known for his exclamation, "Simplify, simplify!" I am afraid that could be misunderstood. One could simplify by repeating the same damned thing over again. The rank layers pile up as you slowly kill yourself.

Thoreau meant that you could earn enough by working only two hours a day as he showed in his Walden (written 1854). That left him great time for his explorations as in being self-appointed as an inspector of snowstorms.

Saint-Exupéry (1971) was of a comparable spirit. He did not think much of adults whom he called "grand personnes." Children were endless explorers like Thoreau. Saint-Exupery dedicated his book to his friend, Leon Werth who remained a child.

Rushdie was a third who could see the world as a child, specifically as a fifteen-year-old boy in his story, The Courter (1994). The boy tells the story of the porter Mixed-Up in his apartment building in London who was misnamed the Courter by his ayah Certainly Mary.

To make a long story short, Mixed-Up the Courter was a chess master who taught Certainly Mary. That was the domain of their love story in which he was indeed the master. However, as porter he kept getting his face bashed in. There he was no master at all, but rather a target for evil bastards.

Noble playing fields are indeed vulnerable. They can be found in smaller playing fields.

Evil bastards have little to gain from crashing in on smaller playing fields. This is what I have to tell you about having such noble fields and defending them. I find them invaluable.

I saw a patient who was a vigorous membership-individual to use a term from Turquet's (1975) long essay on large groups. Being big on membership puts you square in the game of belonging to the club. Is that a good thing? Yes and no. You belong like hell but you are also vulnerable to twenty different illnesses. Why is that? Because you are so rushing ahead to be a big deal that you do not sense the tensions it puts into your body.

Perhaps even worse is being a singleton (Turquet, 1975) because you don't belong at all. Can that be tense for the body also? Also, it is apt to be miserable, having no stage and company of accomplices upon which to act your drama.

Are those the only alternatives? Fortunately, not! The third possibility is what Turquet (1975) called being an individual-member. You belong as a member in good standing, but you also are original in your contributions. Winnicott (1971) was just that kind of doctor. It is an art form to balance membership with originality that can be tolerated by conventional people.

Strangely, nearly fifty years later, we have a host of children about ten years old who are singletons, lacking any friends and companions. What they tend to do is fill up all of their otherwise miserable time with video games.

Feeding this hunger are video game makers whose games can be exceedingly violent. In them you can be a hero by committing suicide or killing other people. Worst of all is that some boys who have no friends imagine doing things like this to be a hero to be respected. The triumph of such a singleton is to do things like hang yourself. Some doctors say they do not mean it. I am not so sure.

Is this not a terrible perversion of play? Certainly it is. Probably it is also feeding an adult society with singleton mass killings all too frequent. One would be too many. I tend now to remain a member but I am not driven by it. I wait to add something original and unthought of if it arises in me. That is play in a constructive sense.

Yes, play is the great origin of originality, but it can also go too far, too daring, too fierce and ask for big trouble. Every virtue (like play) has its opposite. Everything depends on its context. The best novelists know this but psychiatry seems not to know it at all.

When I was twelve years old, on Saturday afternoons, I would go roller-skating at the Brockway Roller Skating Rink for a very small fee. That was sixty-five years ago, but I remember it very well because of a girl who was a very good skater. She always wore an orange kerchief. I was a pretty good skater myself. I kept a distance from her skating with my own. I did not want to alarm her. This was my first passion. I did not go too far, too daring, too fierce. I somehow knew how to refrain from asking for trouble. Of course, all I had was a 1st impression about her. I never had a 2nd impression. As kids do in junior high, I exchanged photographs with her. Then she was gone.

References

Heidegger, M.: *An Introduction to Metaphysics*. New Haven, Connecticut: Yale University Press, 1959.

Huizinga, J.: *Homo Ludens; A Study of the Play-Element in Culture* (1938). Boston: Beacon Press, 1955.

Rushdie, S.: *East, West Stories*. New York: Pantheon Books, 1994.

Saint-Exupéry, A.: *The Little Prince*. New York: Harcourt, Brace, Jovanovich, 1971.

Snow, E.: *A Study of Vermeer*. Berkeley: University of California Press, 1994.

Thoreau, H.: *Walden* (1854). Boston: Shambhala Press, 2004.

Turquet, P.: Threat to identity in the large group in L. Kreeger (Ed.): *Large Group, Dynamics and Therapy*. London: Constable, 1975.

Winnicott, D.W.: *Therapeutic Consultations in Child Psychiatry*. New York: Basic Books, 1971.

15

Religious Deliverance
Light And Dark

Your advantage in reading this final chapter could be a better sense about the lifeline of faith. It is of religious importance, of strength to cope with evil.

As D.W. Winnicott wrote in *Therapeutic Consultations in Childhood Psychiatry* (1971), children have lifelines that they believe in and trust to be true. These lifelines are tested. This makes for strength and resilience. The tests can be overwhelming, however, and the lifelines can be cut. The children can give up.

Adults are no less dependent on their lifelines and vulnerable. Martin Luther King was a remarkable one. From the Birmingham Jail he wrote his letters about being arrested for non-violent protest. We all know he was shot and killed for it.

A patient of mine will serve for a typical example. He retired from his profession, hoping to enjoy spending a lot of time with his wife. Instead he lost all the arguments with her and his lifeline was cut. This was so painful for him that he became manic to rise up out of it and began to walk to Chicago. He was like King Lear in Shakespeare's tragedy by that name. Lear trusted his two older daughters, Goneril and Regan, to take care of him in his stepping down from being king. These two had flattered him most. His youngest daughter, Cordelia, had just said she loved him as a daughter and no more. She was turned away from.

Now when Goneril and Regan turned out to be cruel, Lear's lifeline was cut and his pain great. He fled into the heath, attended by his fool.

Humanity in the Ice Age had a different kind of lifeline. They had to anticipate and make a huge array of transitions, as from wet to dry and hot to cold (Lévi-Strauss, 1964). Theirs had to be a high-dimensional space. It was transmitted orally by their myths.

The end of the Ice Age came with the explosion of one-crop economies: rice or wheat or corn or barley. Harari (2014) called it the "agricultural revolution." This meant you became a specialist like the one-crop farmer or a specialist in one thing in managing these surpluses and defending them from rival armies.

Such lifelines were extremely vulnerable. The one-crop could fail and then would fail the array of specialists who raised, managed and defended them. Disasters ensued.

Moving ahead to more modern times, like the end of the Middle Ages, power took a military form. Jan Kott (1974) called it "the staircase of history." One king would rise to the top of the staircase and get pushed off by the prince behind him. Shakespeare's histories and tragedies run this plot.

Moving ahead to our time, power took the form, as Marx (1867) showed, how this power of capitalists lay in paying their laborers to be reified into things, repeating their thing like any cog in any machine.

This is not totally the case. This is mostly the case. People are paid to repeat themselves endlessly. I have to write my sentence or two, documenting what our residents do. My lifeline too depends upon repeating my function.

I had a patient whose daughter was full of tantrums from age two or three. She took her daughter to a number of therapists. One told the mother her daughter was normal. Another told the mother that unhappy children were not serious enough cases to warrant her time.

Twenty years later this mother came to me because the very same daughter was still having tantrums over the least objection. Evidently, unhappy children are not minor cases. I recalled Winnicott's (1977) small book about helping such children called *The Piggle*. Winnicott helped the piggle in sixteen sessions over three years by having more rage than her! She found him funny and absurd. She let go of tantruming herself.

I had a religious dream screen. A dream screen (Gustafson, 1997, Lewin, 1973) is the surface a dream is enacted upon. In my dream there was a dream screen of a grid of red dots like the red dot on the forehead of a Hindu lady. It was a kind of granular translucent shield with the extraordinary power to intersect with the evil forces of this world and not be swallowed up by them. This would be like the boon captured in the depths by the hero in Joseph Campbell's (1949) monomyth and brought back to the world as strength of one's own that could be shared.

This was accompanied by the music of Tchaikovsky's *5th Symphony* fourth movement that I found exhilarating all night long and into the next day. At the same time, I knew to go slowly the next day, not to be carried away by this triumphant force in acceleration our species is so vulnerable to. Thrill has to have calm as its mate to be well defended.

I am quite sure that strength has to be of religious import to withstand evil. That is why I am concluding my book with the most important finding of all.

The following night I had another dream of religious import about being finished or being able to have rebirth from 2nd impressions. At its start I found myself in a kind of wasteland (T.S. Eliot, 1922) or what Dante (1300) called a dark wood or what Joseph Campbell (1949) called Act I of the monomyth. Here nothing can happen. It just goes around in circles. Things are finished. It is also like the plight of the Jews as captives in Egypt. That was my 1st impression. All I could do is wait in the dark and cold for a 2nd impression.

Before dawn with the slightest light, the 2nd impression came. I found myself stepping on to a basketball court that opened up for me right down the middle. It was like the Red Sea opening up for the Jews to flee to their Promised Land. This is act II of the monomyth, the departure and discovery of the boon.

Act III of the monomyth would be the Promised Land itself, a rebirth. Michael Balint (1968) called it the new beginning. One moves freely. As in air, earth, fire or water.

From being finished to a second birth like William James: Waiting for a 2nd impression allowed it to happen. Having faith it will happen. Many lack this. Thus they are finished.

Kohut (1971) called the help an idealizing transference or a mirroring transference. He called these self-objects. Winnicott (1971) could be both, the ideal dream doctor and the doctor who mirrors who senses what the child feels. Like the child's blanket he or she carries around as a transitional object.

So much depends on what backing the patient got even as an infant. As Winnicott would say, he could sometimes reach to this lifeline and thus bring back to life the child's faith. Not always. He also knew of children who had been knocked down and failed too many times. The two cases can look alike on 1st impression.

I bring up one of the most ancient religious symbols traced back about six thousand years. It is a kind of lifeline. It is called the Vesica Pisces (Erin Curtis, personal communication). It is the intersection of two circles that envelopes the shape of a fish. It is perfectly balanced and brings forth creation. It is forever bringing about rebirth. Thus it is profound and has the power to go slowly into more depth.

I have been studying Henry Beston's great book for the second time. It is about his year on the great beach of Cape Cod. As it says in the Introduction by Robert Finch, the controlling metaphor is the ritual of the Sun, rising slowly in spring, stepping down slowly in summer and sinking slowly into darkness. For him before his cottage, everything in nature on the great beach has to do with the rising and falling of the sun. It is a profound ritual, for which Henry was profoundly grateful. It was the greatest thing he ever witnessed.

Did I not have to ask myself Henry's question? What is the controlling metaphor of my book? You must know it already. It is that everything turns to pivot, or not. This is our fate and the fifteen chapters of my book different kinds of pivoting.

Joseph Campbell (1949) called this ritual the monomyth in three acts. Part I is about being in trouble with no way out of it. Beston (1988) witnessed this countless times in nature around him. Part II is about descending into the depths to find the boon that is saving. Part III is about returning with this boon that indeed saves.

Jung (1963) saw this as a mighty event that could take place only in the religious squared circle called the temenos marked out by the sulcus primigenius. Is that not found in every culture? Not quite. In the modern secular world there is a considerable danger of having no religious depth at all.

Within this ancient context of the Vesica Pisces and Henry Beston's ancient ritual year of the rise and descent of the sun and Joseph Campbell's single myth of heroes with one thousand faces in three acts and Jung's similar descent in the ancient squared circle of the temenos, I had a dream as follows.

About 11 PM in the evening I dreamed of Chaucer's *Canterbury Tales* being refound, some rightly and some not. I did not know what it meant. I wrote it down and went back to sleep.

About 2 AM I dreamed I was a military officer trying to prepare his troops for an onslaught. I placed colored strips where I wanted each of my soldiers to be ready. Then they were to knock out the windows to be able to shoot freely. This made sense on 1st impression.

On 2nd impression pivoting away from the 1st I could see it was a terrible idea. The enemy artillery could slaughter each of us without risking any advance of their troops at all.

I drew a picture of the entire scene. It took place within the sacred framework of the temenos. In it was this dire warning. And from it I could pivot as the captain and get my troops out of this forthcoming hell.

Naturally, I have to ask myself how the analogy or metaphor of this scene is to apply in my present life? It seems to me that it says that religious depth cannot be found everywhere. Rarely is it to be found in psychiatry. The diagnosis of emotional pain is unheard of. Knowing how to get there is very unusual.

In other words, many situations are hell. As my wife said to me, Virgil in the Inferno had to warn Dante (1300) over and over not to look and listen to a denizen of the Inferno for more than a minute or he would pass out. It was too terrible to endure but ever so briefly. To pivot sharply was what Virgil was calling for. Act I of difficulty, Act II of falling into the depths for salvation and Act III of coming back to save oneself: This ran very fast.

I will have to ponder this longer. When I was eight years old in our Congregational Church I had to memorize the 23rd Psalm:

The Lord is my Shepherd. I shall not want. He maketh me to lie down in green pastures; he leadeth me beside the still waters. He restoreth my soul: he leadeth me in the paths of righteousness for his name's sake. Yea though I walk through the valley of the shadow of death I will fear no evil: for thou art with me: thy rod and thy staff they comfort me. Thou prepareth a table before me in the presence of my enemies; thou anointest my head with oil; my cup runneth over. Surely goodness and mercy shall follow me all of the days of my life and I shall dwell in the house of the Lord forever.

The metaphor of being a sheep entirely watched over by a Shepherd was very comforting when I was eight years old. As I got older, I saw that I had to watch out for myself about the situation as a whole.

Tate argued that there are three types of poetry (1934). The first is scientific will such as how to dig an oil well and extract the oil with no consideration for the land. The second is romantic will that revolts against the domination of science to have its own metaphors that owe nothing to science. Shelley was a leading example. The third is nameless because it is perfect, because it is complete and whole as in Shakespeare.

To me scientific will and romantic will are dangerous to an adult. Such perspectives of the part falsify their whole situation. I need to read the whole situation to be prepared to meet it. That is my faith and my lifeline. It is to see broadly and deeply. The surface and the façade yield 1st impressions. I note them and pivot for 2nd impressions that will take in the whole situation.

I dreamed of three places that made no sense. Jung called that the reduction to absurdity. It is the opposite of sacred depth.

How did I recall my dream in my book (Gustafson, 2000) of the Ausable River (in Michigan where I grew up, Ausable means black) where my dream built a Cathedral with the river of light running through the transept of the Cathedral? My father and my uncle carrying spades were digging out the silt of the nave to let in the light. It was truly a sacred deliverance of light from the darkness.

How did this kick off my memory of light in the darkness that was a snare for Agamemnon? I remembered Gilchrist's essay (2013) about being snared by light in the darkness as a huge theme in Greek tragedy like the Oresteia of Aeschylus.

In other words, light in the darkness can be a sacred signal of being saved or a hellish signal of being lured into the light to be destroyed. One cannot know for sure on 1st impressions and must wait for 2nd impressions, or perhaps as in *Agamemnon* a double take for the watchman that he was glad Agamemnon was returning, but also that he dreaded at the same moment that Agamemnon was only coming to be murdered by his wife and her lover.

"Lean towards the light but having silent knowledge of abominations." Joseph Campbell said that (Stuart Jones, personal communication). Certainly abominations have the ring of the Old Testament, that which was impure and disgusting and hated by God.

Is abomination not a larger category than evil? For example, in our modern times, increase packs are preoccupied with making as many copies of something as possible with an eye to having as much credit as possible. That is what Marcuse (1964) called one-dimensional man. Is that hardly a life? Will it sustain meaning? I doubt it. Is it abominable? To my ear it sounds like something I do not want to do.

References

Balint, M.: *The Basic Fault, Therapeutic Aspects of Regression*. London: Tavistock Press, 1968.

Beston, H.: *The Outermost House, A Year of Life on the Great Beach of Cape Cod*. New York: St. Martin's Griffin, 1988.

Campbell, J.: *The Hero with a Thousand Faces*. Princeton, New Jersey: Princeton: University Press, 1949.

Gilchrist, T.: Darkness, light and drama in the Oresteia. *Reed Magazine*, December 2013.

Gustafson, J.: *The New Interpretation of Dreams*. Madison, Wisconsin: James Gustafson Publisher, 1997.

Gustafson, J.: *The Practical Use of Dreams and the Human Comedy*. Madison, Wisconsin: James Gustafson Publisher, 2000.

Harari, Y.: *Sapiens, A Brief History of Mankind*. New York: Harper, 2014.

Jung, C.: *Memories, Dreams and Reflections*. New York: Vintage Books, 1963.

Kohut, H.: *The Analysis of the Self*. New York: International Universities Press, 1971.

Kott, J.: *Shakespeare, Our Contemporary*. New York: W.W. Norton, 1974.

Lévi-Strauss, C.: *The Raw and the Cooked, Mythologique*, Part I. Chicago: University of Chicago Press, 1964.

Lewin, B.: *Selected Writings of Bertram D. Lewin*. New York: Psychoanalytic Quarterly Press, 1973.

Marcuse, H.: *One-Dimensional Man*. Boston: Beacon, 1964.

Marx, K.: *Capital, Critique of Political Economy* (in German). Verlag von Otto Meisner, Hamburg, 1867.

Tate, A.: Three Types of Poetry (1934) in *Essays of Four Decades*. Wilmington, Delaware: ISI Books, 1999.

Winnicott, D.W.: *Therapeutic Consultations in Child Psychiatry*. New York: Basic Books, 1971.

Winnicott, D.W.: *The Piggle, An Account of the Psychoanalytic Treatment of a Little Girl*. London: Penguin Books, 1977.

Afterword

Your ultimate advantage in reading this book could be to adopt this procedure of not being beguiled by the surfaces of 1st impressions and then wait until you can pivot to 2nd impressions.

A generality like that sentence needs to picture an example. Sixty years ago when I played basketball on the MIT freshman team, we had a bastard of a coach who did nothing but scream at us and jerk us out when we made the slightest mistake. We could not play, always looking over our shoulders to take in this guy's eye. We were tight. So many people live like that in hell. In that context nothing new can happen, no spontaneity, no ingenuity and no risks. Wilhelm Reich (1933) called it a constant attitude that sets up a character armor that gets more and more rigid.

Fortunately, for one evening, against Harvard, the assistant coach, a real basketball player from Kentucky just let us five play. We did, pivoting and wheeling freely, and nearly won in double overtime, except I broke my ankle in the first overtime and did not tell our coach.

Sherwood Anderson would have understood this perfectly. In his novel, *Winesburg Ohio* (1919) he described an entire town of lost souls looking over their own shoulders to do the one thing they knew how to do. They were all tight, becoming more rigid, afraid of rejection or being taken out of the game.

Now you know what will be locked in forever, versus what can freely pivot to make original moves.

References

Anderson, S.: *Winesburg, Ohio* (1919). New York: Viking Press, 1960.
Reich, W.: *Character Analysis* (1933). New York: Farrar, Straus and Giroux, 1949.

Index

Aristotle 21

Bateson, G. 12
Beston, H. 37, 47, 88, 108
Bible (23rd Psalm) 109
Binswanger, L. 27

Campbell, J. 106–107, 110
catastrophe theory 80
Curtis, E. 107

Dante 109
Donovan, J. 47
downward going man 29

Engel, G. 9
Erikson, E. 50

Freire, P. 85
Freud, S. 4, 46

gates of ivory, gates of horn 45–46

Harari, Y. 57, 106
Hardy, T. 21
Homer 45–46
Hoyt, M. 35
Hughes, T. 36
Huizinga, J. 101

Ibsen, H. 22

James, W. 38, 61
Jones, S. 58, 85, 110
Jung, C. 50–52, 108

Lévi-Strauss, C. 46, 58–59, 105
lifelines 16, 105, 106

Margulies, A. 47, 50, 52–53
Marx, K. 106
McCarthy, C. 55, 69

Poincaré, H. 65–66

Reich, W. 4, 110

security operations 31
Shakespeare, W. 58, 87, 105, 109
Shirley, J. 97
Simoneau, G. 13, 35, 89
Stevenson, R.L. 29
Sullivan, H.S. 4–5, 11, 15, 31, 59

Thom, R. 80
Tolstoy, L. 95

unknown unknowns 28

Wilson, E.O. 73
Winnicott, D.W. 5–6, 16, 59, 103, 105, 107
Wood, M. 14, 31

Yeats, W.B. 27

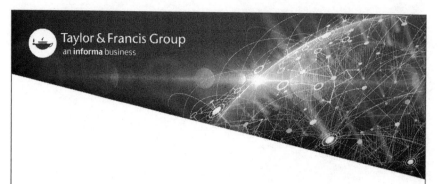